Freeing the Heart and Mind

Freeing the Heart and Mind

Part Three: *Teachings of the Sakya Path*

His Holiness Kyabgon Gongma
Sakya Trichen Rinpoche

Wisdom

Wisdom Publications
199 Elm Street
Somerville, MA 02144 USA
wisdomexperience.org

Library of Congress Cataloging-in-Publication Data
Names: Ngag-dbang-kun-dga'-theg-chen-dpal-'bar, Sa-skya Khri-'dzin XLI, 1945– author.
Title: Freeing the heart and mind. Part 3, Teachings of the Sakya path / His Holiness Kyabgon Gongma, Sakya Trichen Rinpoche.
Description: Somerville, MA, USA: Wisdom Publications, 2020.
Identifiers: LCCN 2019045354 (print) | LCCN 2019045355 (ebook) | ISBN 9781614296331 (paperback) | ISBN 9781614296348 (ebook)
Subjects: LCSH: Sa-skya-pa (Sect)
Classification: LCC BQ7672.2 .N43 2020 (print) | LCC BQ7672.2 (ebook) | DDC 294.3/420423—dc23
LC record available at https://lccn.loc.gov/2019045354
LC ebook record available at https://lccn.loc.gov/2019045355

ISBN 978-1-61429-633-1 ebook ISBN 978-1-61429-634-8

24 23 22 21 20
5 4 3 2 1

Cover photo by Tan Hui Chuan. Cover design by Marc Whitaker. Interior design by Gopa & Ted 2 and Tony Lulek.
Typeset by Tony Lulek. Set in DGP 11.25/14.56.

Printed on acid-free paper and meets the guidelines for permanence and durability of the Production Guidelines for Book Longevity of the Council on Library Resources.

Printed in the United States of America.

Contents

Part Four: Dharma in Present Lives, Future Lives, and the World

Preface

THIS BOOK INCLUDES a variety of Dharma teachings that I have given in various places at different times, which have been collected and edited by my students. I hope that it will be useful to those who are interested in the Buddhadharma in general, especially those engaged in Dharma study who seek practical advice on how to practice the path.

The great master Vasubandhu wrote, "Observe moral discipline, and after studying and contemplating the teachings, apply oneself intensively to meditation." Dharma study, contemplation, and practice is the most useful thing that we can do with our lives.

Everyone wishes for and seeks happiness, but until we have made spiritual progress, we cannot actually gain the happiness we seek. All other external worldly goals will bring more misery and suffering, instead of more happiness—unless they are linked to inner mental development. Thus, Dharma study and practice is the best way to find temporary happiness in this and future lives, and to eventually attain Buddhahood.

Many thanks to Venerable Khenpo Kalsang Gyaltsen, Chodrungma Kunga Chodron, Jon Mark Fletcher, and Kyle Garton-Gundling at Tsechen Kunchab Ling in Walden, New York, for collecting and editing these Dharma talks, with the support of the Sachen Foundation and other generous sponsors. I also appreciate the expert assistance of Laura Cunningham and other team members at Wisdom Publications who prepared the chapters for publication.

Part One

The Buddhist Path

1. The Four Noble Truths

IN THIS WORLD, there are many different places, cultures, philosophies, religions, and traditions. But one thing common to all of them is that everybody wants to be free from suffering. In other words, everybody wishes to have happiness. Every individual is making efforts in their community and every country is making efforts in the world toward this goal.

But it is very clear that until we have made spiritual progress, we cannot actually gain the happiness we are seeking, no matter how much external effort we put forth or how much progress we make. Although the fundamental goal is to achieve happiness, every external goal, unless it is linked to inner mental development, will in fact bring more misery and suffering instead of bringing more happiness. Therefore, everyone's goal of true happiness has to come through inner spiritual development. It is only through spiritual practices that we can achieve happiness.

There are many great masters who came into this world and gave many different types of teachings. Each teaching has its own beauty, its own ways to solve problems, and its own path to find inner peace and happiness. But what I will discuss is the path according to the Lord Buddha Śākyamuni.

For three countless eons, the Buddha worked to accumulate tremendous amounts of merit and wisdom for the benefit of sentient beings. Through that accumulation of merit and wisdom, he eventually overcame all obscurations and defilements. Everything that needed to be parted from was parted from and every possible good quality that needed to be gained was gained.

The Buddha is fully awakened, fully enlightened, and has the power to help sentient beings free themselves from suffering. Even one ray of light from his body or one line of his teaching can help countless sentient beings in a single moment. Directly or indirectly, any contact with the Buddha will help to release one from suffering and gain happiness.

From the beginning, the Buddha's whole purpose was to help all sentient beings without any exception. Every activity that he performed was for the benefit of sentient beings. He performed many great physical activities, verbal activities, and mental activities. But among these, the most important were his verbal activities: the teachings he gave about what he had realized. This is called "turning the wheel of Dharma." Through these teachings, the Buddha helps sentient beings. Those who are not ripe are ripened, those who are not on the path are placed on the path, those who are not making progress become able to make progress, and those who are already making progress are helped to gain higher realization.

Sentient beings have no limit—they are countless, just as space is limitless. These limitless sentient beings are all different—their mentalities, their defilements, their mental conditions, their propensities are all different. Therefore, one type of teaching cannot help all sentient beings. Just as there are different types of medicines and treatments in order to cure different types of diseases, the Buddha gave an enormous number of teachings in order to suit every type of sentient being. So the teachings of the Buddha have many different levels, according to the followers' mental states and conditions, situations, environments, and so forth.

In this chapter we are going to focus on what is known as "the first turning of the wheel of Dharma." This teaching occurred after the Buddha attained enlightenment at Sarnath (Deer Park). The subject of that first teaching is the four noble truths. The four noble truths include both the cause and result of saṃsāra, and the cause and result of nirvāṇa. The four noble truths are (1) the truth of suffering, (2) the truth of the cause of suffering, (3) the truth of cessation, and (4) the truth of the path. One must know the truth of suffering, abstain from the cause of suffering, realize the truth of cessation, and practice the truth of the path.

The Truth of Suffering

First, one should know the truth of suffering. If we are sick with a specific disease, the first thing we must do is to learn the exact nature of the sickness. Otherwise, we cannot determine any treatments. Similarly, to have an effective treatment for suffering, one must know the exact nature of suffering. In order to give rise to genuine renunciation thought, which is the sincere wish to practice and enter the path in order to gain liberation, we must know the truth of suffering, what suffering is, and the exact nature of suffering.

As long as we are in saṃsāra, we are not free from suffering. According to the teachings, saṃsāra is divided into six realms: three lower realms and three higher realms. The three lower realms are the hell realm, the hungry ghost realm, and the animal realm. The hell realm and the hungry ghost realm are not directly visible to us. Instead, we learn about their nature and characteristics from the sūtras and from the authentic commentaries. But the animal realm is visible to us, and we can easily see how animals suffer. The three higher realms are the human realm, the demigod realm, and the god realm. In these realms, there appears to be a mixture of happiness and suffering. However, if we carefully examine them, we find that there is no real happiness. It is only when we compare an experience to great suffering that it will appear as happiness. When we think carefully, however, we can see that even the experiences we consider to be happiness are, in reality, another kind of suffering.

Generally speaking, there are three different types of suffering: (1) the suffering of suffering, (2) the suffering of change, and (3) the suffering of the conditional nature of all things.

The suffering of suffering is visible suffering, the suffering we consider to be suffering, such as physical pain, mental anxiety, and so on. This suffering is most prevalent in the lower realms. The main cause of rebirth in the three lower realms is ignorance.

The hell realm has so much suffering. There are hot hells, cold hells, neighboring hells, and so on. The greatest suffering experienced by human beings cannot represent even the slightest part of hell-realm suffering.

Beings are born in hell due to their karma, particularly the karma related to anger and hatred.

The second lower realm is that of hungry ghosts. This realm exists mainly due to desire and attachment, resulting in stinginess. Thus, beings who fall into the hungry ghost realm experience extreme hunger and thirst; for ages those hungry ghosts cannot find even a single drop of water. There are three types of hungry ghost realms: those where beings have (1) outer obscurations, (2) inner obscurations, and (3) obscuration of obscurations.

In the animal realm, we can actually see how much beings suffer. No human being could bear even the slightest part of the suffering that animals go through. Animals in the jungle, animals in the ocean, animals belonging to humans, animals not belonging to humans—all of these are either tortured or killed. Animals have to remain in constant fear.

Then there are three higher realms: (1) the human realm, (2) the demigod realm, and (3) the god realm. First of all, no one in the human realm is free from the four sufferings—the sufferings of birth, old age, sickness, and death. And there are also many other types of suffering in the human realm—the suffering of meeting enemies, the suffering of losing friends, the suffering of not fulfilling one's wishes, and the suffering of undesirable things happening. Those who are poor suffer from being unable to find food, clothing, shelter, medicine, and so on. On the other hand, those who are rich have many mental burdens and sufferings of their own. No matter what one does, there is no satisfaction. Whatever we do, in spite of all the efforts we make to eliminate suffering and to gain happiness, we cannot find our actual goal of happiness.

In the human realm, beings experience some suffering of suffering, as described for the lower realms, but their primary suffering is the suffering of change. Everything is changing: large families lose members, gradually dwindle down to one single member, and then disappear; the rich become poor and the poor become rich; people with power become weak; and so on. Everything is changing.

The demigod realm is higher than the human realm but lower than the god realm; therefore, its inhabitants are called "demigods." The demigods are naturally envious because they are constantly engaged in wars with the gods and other demigods. Since their power is not equivalent to the power of the gods, they are constantly defeated. Due to this, they have much physical and mental suffering.

In the first god realm, known as *kāmadhātu*, the gods have a very luxurious life; everything prospers; there they have all the worldly good qualities such as long life, good health, and an abundance of food. But because of this, their whole lives are spent in leisure and enjoyment. They do not realize how quickly their lives are passing, and only when the signs of death appear do they start to think of how they have spent their whole lives in wasteful luxury and now have to fall into the lower realms. Therefore, they have tremendous mental suffering at the time of death. This type of suffering is even greater than the physical suffering in the lower realms.

Then there are the highest deva realms, which are known as the *rūpadhātu*, the form realm, and the *arūpadhātu*, or formless realm. In these realms, beings don't have physical suffering as we have here. They possess very high meditational states, but these are worldly meditational states that have not yet cut the root of suffering, which is self-clinging; they do not have the wisdom to dig out the root of samsaric suffering. Therefore, after remaining for a long time in a meditative state, they again fall down into the lower realms, like birds. No matter how high they fly in the sky, eventually they have to land on the ground. Likewise, beings in the form and formless realms go to the highest worldly stage and then fall back into the lower realms.

All of this is saṃsāra, the realm of existence. It is suffering from the highest deva stage to the lowest hell realm. It is completely permeated by the three types of sufferings.

Everything is changing; anything that is gained through causes and conditions is impermanent. If it is impermanent, it is suffering because it does not remain. For example, today we do not have so much physical suffering. We are healthy and able-bodied—but anything can happen at any moment. Therefore, we experience the suffering of change, including the change from feeling happy to feeling unhappy.

And then there is the suffering of the conditional nature of all things: no matter how much we work, how many actions we perform, or how much effort we make, there is no end. From birth until now, we have engaged in many different actions and types of work, but we have never finished them and never feel satisfied. For anything we start, there is no satisfactory end. Like the food we eat, the more we eat, the more we desire; this is suffering. No matter where one is, from the lowest realm to the highest realm, saṃsāra is completely full of suffering. Like the nature of fire is hot whether it is a small fire or big, the nature of saṃsāra is suffering whether in the lower realms or the higher realms.

We must first know this in order to overcome these limitations. To know the nature of suffering is very important. It is important not only to try to understand suffering intellectually but actually to feel it, until you are deeply moved to be permanently free from the realms of existence.

The Truth of the Cause of Suffering

In the first noble truth, the Buddha taught that one must know the truth of suffering. The second noble truth is the cause of suffering. For example, when we are sick, we must know the exact nature of the disease not only so that we can take the proper treatment but also so that we can avoid the cause of the disease. If we take the treatment but continue to expose ourselves to the cause of the disease, we will not be able to cure it. Therefore, the second stage is to abstain from the cause of suffering.

What is the cause of suffering? The cause of suffering is actually actions and defilements. Where do defilements come from? They come from ignorance, from self-clinging. Our mind's true nature is pure but we do not recognize this; instead we cling to a "self" without authentic reasons and logic. We cling to our overall existence; we mistakenly believe that our being exists as a self.

When you have a self, then automatically you have an other. Self and other depend on each other. When you have self and other, then there is attachment to one's own friends and relatives and so forth. And there is also the other side—the people you do not like, beings that you do not appreciate, beings that you do not agree with, etc., and so anger arises. From ignorance comes both desire and hatred.

In this way, the defilements are formed, which are known as the three main poisons: ignorance, desire, and hatred. These three give rise to the other defilements. For instance, when you have attachment to your wealth and possessions, then you generate stinginess and pride. And when other people have wealth and prosperity, you then have jealousy and competitiveness and so forth. All of these impure mental states arise.

Based on these impure mental states, you then take actions—physical actions, mental actions, and verbal actions. These actions are like planting a seed of suffering. Actions that arise from the defilements are all forms of suffering. If the root of a tree is poisonous, then anything that grows on the tree, such as fruits, flowers, and leaves, are all poisonous. Similarly, the actions arising from defilements—ignorance, hatred, and desire—are all nonvirtuous deeds and are the cause of suffering. Performing an action is like planting a seed. When you plant a seed, its fruit depends on causes and conditions. When the right causes and conditions are brought together, then you are bound to produce a result. Through our own actions, we have created all of our own situations. Through all of our own actions, we have created our own suffering. It is through all our own actions that we have created all of our happiness. Everything comes from our own actions.

Therefore, the Buddha said that the second truth is to abstain from the cause of suffering, which is the defilements. When you wish to be free from suffering, then you must abstain from its cause. But if you continuously create the cause, then the result of suffering is bound to follow. These first two truths show that everything in saṃsāra arises out of our own actions, from our own defilements, and through our own self-clinging. As a result, we are born in saṃsāra, which is full of suffering. So the first truth is the result and the second truth is the cause.

The Truth of Cessation

The third noble truth is the truth of cessation. When you are sick, you seek to recover from the disease and become healthy. Similarly, what we are seeking is to be free from suffering.

Nobody else can remove your suffering. Each person has to work their own way out of suffering. The Buddha said, "You yourself are you own savior." Nobody else can save you; only you can save yourself. For example, when a person is sick, although it is very important to have a good doctor, good medicine, and good helpers, the main factor is that the patient themself has to take the medicine and abstain from the cause of the disease. Otherwise, no matter how good the doctor or how good the medicine, the patient will never get well. Similarly, the Buddha is like a doctor and the Dharma is like medicine—together, they help us to be free from suffering.

Even though we receive help in the form of the Buddha's blessing, compassion, and grace, due to our own faults and defilements, we have not yet been able to relieve ourselves from the suffering of saṃsāra.

Among the sentient beings of the six realms, we human beings are endowed with superior knowledge and intelligence so we can work effectively to free ourselves from suffering. Even animals can do this to a degree. But we are different from animals; we have intelligence, we have a mind to think, and we have the capability to overcome all of our problems. Therefore, we must not lose precious time.

What we are seeking is the state beyond suffering. Therefore, the Buddha spoke of "the truth of cessation, which one must obtain." That is the goal we are seeking: the state that is permanently free, the state where we have permanently parted from all types of suffering and there can be no more relapse. In such a state, we are not only free from suffering, but suffering never reoccurs.

The Truth of the Path

How do we get to the state of complete cessation of suffering? The truth of the path is the cause of attaining the state permanently free of suffering. Therefore, it is said that the fourth noble truth is the truth of the path that we must practice.

Again, if we are sick, in order to be cured and completely recover from sickness, we must receive treatment. Similarly, the truth of the path is what we must practice. As I said before, one must accomplish this oneself, so you must turn to yourself for help. The Buddha said, "I have shown the path of liberation, and whether you attain enlightenment or not depends on yourself." Thus, we have to practice.

How, then, should we practice? We must eliminate our defilements—such as anger, hatred, desire, pride, and stinginess—through different methods and practices, such as meditations and contemplations on loving-kindness and compassion, breathing practices, concentration practices, interdependent origination practices, and so on. There are so many different types of meditations and methods.

Through these meditations, we reduce or suppress the impure mental states that are causing nonvirtuous actions, and we develop the positive qualities of our mind that eliminate these impure mental states. Yet this method alone yields only temporary results.

The main thing that we must do is to attain wisdom, the wisdom of cutting the root of saṃsāra. The root of saṃsāra is the ignorance that does not realize selflessness. The root of all suffering is self-clinging. From this self-clinging arises all impurities in the mind, and due to it, all nonvirtuous actions are undertaken. Then we suffer. Therefore, the root of suffering is self-clinging. To overcome this self-clinging, we must develop the wisdom of selflessness. It is the complete opposite of self-clinging. If we search for this self to which we mistakenly cling, we cannot find it. There are many reasons that this is true.

Our mind is constantly engaged in many different thoughts, so we cannot meditate on insight wisdom straight away. In order to become able to meditate, the first thing we have to do is to improve our concentration. Concentrate on a specific object with your mind and then focus on the breath. The eyes focus on the meditative object and remain there, instead of thinking about its color and shape and so on. Remain in this state as it is. There are many other methods—such as remembering the types of concentrations, applying the antidotes, practicing various methods of concentration, etc.—that try to bring the mind to concentrate on the object. In the beginning, when doing this, more thoughts seem to come. This is not only our normal stream of thoughts, but it feels like even more than usual. This is because normally we do not discipline our mind and pay attention to our thoughts. When you try to meditate, then you start to notice your thoughts. This is the first sign of improvement. Then the number and duration of your thoughts will slowly be reduced, and then eventually your mind will become able to remain completely single-pointed, free of thoughts, like an ocean without waves.

The base of this ability is clarity of mind. This is attained through proper concentration. Only after we attain clarity of mind can we meditate on insight wisdom. Through very sharp reasoning, we logically analyze teachings that explain how everything is devoid of self, and we see that the truth is not in any extreme. The perfection of wisdom is to thus awaken from all forms of extremes and elaborations.

The last two truths—the truth of cessation and the truth of the path—are the cause and result of nirvāṇa. The Buddha taught these four noble truths at the very beginning; they were his first teaching. This teaching is shared by all the Buddhist traditions. Through them, we turn away from nonvirtuous actions and establish ourselves on the right path. After putting ourselves on the right path, we pursue the path further to gain liberation.

2. Preliminary Practices and Their Importance

In our lives as human beings, many things are required of us, and we engage in many kinds of activities. But the most important thing we can do in our lives is spiritual practice, which allows us to accomplish peace and happiness not only in this life but also in future lives. The Buddha's teaching says that every sentient being possesses buddha nature. All sentient beings, and not only human beings, possess buddha nature, which is the seed or potential to become buddhas, so that if we meet with the right methods we can accomplish buddhahood. In this sense, then, everyone is equal. I feel that the Buddha was the first person to pronounce equal rights, and not only for human beings but for every sentient being, and he did so on this basis.

But at the moment, we do not realize our buddha nature. We cannot see the true nature of our mind because of the two obscurations: the obscuration of defilements and the obscuration of knowledge. Due to this great ignorance or lack of wisdom, we cling without any logical reason to the idea of a self rather than seeing the true nature of our mind. And as a result of the buildup of strong habitual tendencies, accumulated over a very long period of time, we cling to our aggregates as a self. When you cling to "self," then naturally there are "others." When you have self and others, there is attachment to your side, anger toward others, and ignorance in general. From these three arise pride, jealousy, stinginess, and so on. This array of defilements drives us to action, or karma, and due to our actions, we are caught up in what we call saṃsāra, or the circle of existence. This pattern goes on and on, and so it is called "the circle of life" or "the wheel of life." A wheel turns one round and then another, and it does not stop. Like a wheel, we are born here, go through this life, and then we die and begin our next life.

Of course, there is the question of whether there is a next life in the first place. Some people say that there is, and some people say that we do not know. Many people believe that there is no such thing as a next life because we do not see it. However, we can infer a next life because of the difference between the body and the mind.

The body is visible. We know where it comes from, how it is formed, how it grows, and how it is sustained. We can see it with our eyes, touch it with our hands, and describe its color, size, shape, and so on. Eventually, of course, this body will be disposed of in one way or another.

The mind is something different. We cannot see it with our eyes, touch it with our hands, or describe its color, size, or shape. The mind is something else altogether, something invisible. Even so, the mind is more powerful. The physical body will not function without the mind. A body without a mind is a dead body. The mind is the most important determinant of all good things and all bad things, all virtuous deeds and all nonvirtuous deeds. When we die, our bodies will be disposed of in one way or another, but the mind cannot be washed or cremated or buried. Because it is invisible, it cannot disappear. And if it cannot disappear, then it must enter another life. This is the logical argument to establish that the mind continues from life to life.

Once we can establish that there will be a next life, the question arises: From whence did our present mind come? And this allows us to establish that there was a previous life. In this way, we learn to see that the cycle of life goes on and on.

Throughout saṃsāra, everyone is suffering. Of course, in poor countries, there is great physical suffering from things like hunger and poverty. In developed countries, too, as everyone can see, people are still not satisfied, even though we have many facilities. There are always problems and things to complain about. This shows us that all of saṃsāra is suffering. Whether you are a believer or a nonbeliever, whatever your religion, philosophy, or ideology, everyone can agree that no one wants suffering and everyone is longing for happiness. For the sake of happiness, we develop our nation's infrastructure. For the sake of happiness, we practice. For the sake of happiness, too, we do bad things, hoping that by doing this or that, we might gain a certain kind of happiness. Everything that people do is for the sake of happiness.

But we cannot achieve real happiness by exerting ourselves in making material progress. This is obvious. The only way to achieve real happiness and peace is through spiritual practices that change the mind. In religious teachings, we can find such practices. There are many different religions in the world, and I believe that every religion has its own beauty and its own ways to help humankind. People are different, and a variety of spiritualities is necessary.

Since I am a Buddhist, I speak from a Buddhist point of view. Buddhists teach that the way to achieve real peace and happiness is through the practice of what we call Dharma. The word *dharma* in Sanskrit has many different meanings in different contexts, but when we refer to the holy Dharma, we refer to the teachings of the Buddha—teachings that have the power to change our mind.

If we were to claim that the Buddha is great just because of his own majesty, we would not really be establishing that the Buddha is great. Instead, we first look to the teachings that the Buddha gave. Then, when we practice them, we gain experience. The Dharma changes our mental attitude. It gives us the strength to face problems and to develop spiritually. It is on this basis that we say that the teacher is great. The one who has given such a great teaching must be a great religious founder.

According to the Buddha's teachings, the only way to overcome suffering is to practice the Dharma. To do this, you need a base upon which to develop. This base is buddha nature. Every sentient being has buddha nature, which means that every sentient being who meets with the right methods can become a buddha.

Among beings, human beings have the best chance of doing so. The lower realms have unimaginable amounts of suffering and ignorance, such that there is absolutely no chance for them to practice the Dharma. In the higher realms, the demigods and the gods have much greater attributes—better places, better bodies, longer lives, and generally a far better world than the one that human beings experience. But the human realm involves aspects of both the higher and the lower realms in an opportune combination. We have the leisure, the freedom, and the chance to practice the Dharma, and, at the same time, we have suffering that helps lead us to the spiritual path. In this way, in terms of a base upon which to practice the Dharma, a human life is best.

This human life is very difficult to obtain, especially a human life endowed with all the prerequisites for spiritual practice. A human life, free from unfavorable conditions and possessing favorable conditions, is very difficult to obtain from many points of view: from a numerical point of view, from the cause point of view, from the example point of view, and from the nature point of view. From a numerical point of view, for instance, it seems at first glance that there are very many human beings, so many that some parts of the world have the problem of overpopulation. But when you compare the number of humans to other living beings, the number of human beings is not so great. It is possible to count how many people live in a given country, for example, but it is very difficult to count how many insects live in even a single house.

Not only is a human rebirth difficult to obtain, it is also very precious. A human rebirth is more precious than what we call a wish-fulfilling jewel. It is said that there is a special jewel that can fulfill all of your wishes if you clean it and put it in a high place. This jewel can bestow all of your material needs, like food, shelter, medicine, clothes, and so on. However, it cannot bestow liberation or enlightenment, or even a higher rebirth. This human life is more precious than a wish-fulfilling jewel, because based upon this human life we can accomplish a higher rebirth, liberation, and even ultimate enlightenment.

Thus we can see that this human life is exceptionally precious. Due to our own merit, virtuous deeds, and special prayers, we have been born as human beings free from all the unfavorable conditions, and we have attained a life that has all the favorable conditions.

We should take advantage of such a rare and precious opportunity. We cannot be sure that we will have such an opportunity in the next life. Therefore, while we have the chance, we should make the most of it. We must try to practice and to gain at least some steps toward liberation and enlightenment. Liberation and enlightenment are not things that anyone can give you like a gift or bestow upon you as a result of your prayers.

The way that the Buddha helped sentient beings was not by performing miracles or by helping with his hands, but rather by showing us the right direction. He said, "This is the right way, and that is the wrong way. If you go that way, you are going to suffer. But if you go this way, then you will be freed from suffering." The Buddha has shown us the path, but to reach the destination we ourselves have to travel there. The Buddha cannot transport us there. We have to make the journey ourselves.

Therefore, having all the opportunities that we are born with as human beings, and having all the necessary conditions, we should not waste them. We must capitalize on our opportunity quickly, because one can never know when this life will end. The Buddha said that all compounded things are impermanent. Compounded things means things that are created through causes and conditions. All such things are impermanent.

It is said that the end of gathering is separation. Whenever we gather for an event, it is easy to see that eventually we will all go separately in our respective directions. But we often think of other types of gatherings—like family, for example—as permanent. They are also only temporary. No one lives forever. Furthermore, the end of accumulation is exhaustion. No matter the amount of wealth, possessions, material things, and power you accumulate, these things do not last forever. Eventually they are all exhausted.

The end of rising high is falling. No matter what height you reach, you will eventually fall. History tells us that in ancient times there were universal emperors who conquered many continents. Even in modern history, there are empires that have owned almost the entire world. But they do not last forever. Eventually, they all lose territory until they are very small. Thus the end of rising high is falling.

Finally, the end of birth is death. Any life form that is born into this world must end with death. There is no one who is born who does not die. There is not even the slightest doubt about this. We read histories of great masters who were very holy, who devoted their entire lives to the benefit of other sentient beings. But today even those great ones are just historical figures. There are also great statesmen, great emperors, great leaders, our own ancestors, and so on. There have been many great people who today no longer exist. And one hundred years from now, no one who is reading this will remain in this world. Therefore, the end of birth is death.

Furthermore, no one can tell us when our death will come. There is complete uncertainty about when death will take us. Although there are divinations, astrological predictions, and prophecies that might tell you that you are going to live for a certain number of years, there is no certainty in this. For example, consider a lit candle. Although the candle may be very tall and shining brightly, a gust of wind can blow it out at any moment. Similarly, outward events like accidents, heart attacks, and other things can overtake us.

Internally, our physical body is made up of elements like heat, water, and so on. When the elements are balanced, we are healthy and happy. But if the elements are unbalanced, the body becomes disturbed, and all kinds of pain and sickness can arise. Certain diseases can also arise from eating bad food. All of these considerations illustrate that there is no definite lifespan. Therefore, it is very important to use this precious life in the most effective way so that it is not wasted. This life should be used in a purposeful way, for the sake of the highest benefit to oneself and all beings. We can best do this through practicing the spiritual path, so that we can reach at least certain steps toward liberation and enlightenment.

Today we find that many people are interested in the Dharma path, and many people follow a set of associated traditions. We go to temples, do prostrations, recite prayers and mantras, make offerings, perform circumambulations, and do meditations. All of this is of course very meritorious. But these practices alone are not truly effective unless we are making inner mental changes.

First, we have to think, "What is the most important thing in life?" Many people want nothing more than higher positions, wealth, fame, friends, and supporters. But all of this worldly prosperity has no ultimate purpose. In the human realm, very few people attain an age of even one hundred years. Our lifetime is just a matter of, at most, one hundred years. And after that, our worldly attainments will not matter. On the day that you leave this world, no matter how clever you are, how powerful you are, how rich you are, how many supporters you have, or how many friends you have, none of these will help. We must die by ourselves, alone. Nobody can share that suffering or prevent it for us.

The only thing that will help at that moment is our Dharma practice. The virtuous deeds that we do can help us at that moment, and for this reason it is very important to perform positive actions right now, while we can. You never know whether or not you will have an opportunity to practice in the future. Many people think, "At the moment, I am young, so for the time being, I will enjoy life, and then when I get older, I will enter the spiritual path." But there are many young people who die before very old people. Many healthy people die before people who are very sick. Truly, no one can ever tell when they will die. Therefore, it is important to begin the spiritual path right away and then to practice it very diligently.

Although we may perform many practices associated with the Dharma, I feel that far too often we are not truly thinking about them. We just do what others are doing. In particular, among those of us who traditionally follow the Dharma, we often simply imitate others, thinking, "All of these people are going to the temple and praying, and I will too." But we are not really thinking about why we are practicing the Dharma, about the benefit of practicing the Dharma, about the consequences of not practicing the Dharma, and so on. This is why I think, first of all, that it is very important for us to consider, "What is the most important thing in life? How can we achieve real peace and happiness?" Reflecting on these questions, we realize that the only way to achieve real peace and happiness is to practice the Dharma.

How, then, can we practice the Dharma? True Dharma practice is not just praying or going to temples or making offerings, doing prostrations, or performing circumambulations. True Dharma practice is changing our mind. If you recite many prayers, recite many mantras, and do lots of circumambulations, of course this is meritorious; these actions add up and they are very virtuous deeds through which you can earn great merit. But if your mind remains unchanged, that alone will not accomplish liberation or enlightenment.

To change our mind, it is essential that we do such preliminary practices as contemplating the suffering of saṃsāra, the difficulties of obtaining a precious human birth, impermanence, and the law of karma, or cause and effect. By contemplating these things, we begin to think, "Why are we here? Why do we have to go through this life with all its sufferings? Why do we have to suffer? Who is doing all this? Why must we toil through so many different kinds of experiences that we encounter?" In response to these questions, the Buddha said that everything is created by our own karma. There is no outside creator who is responsible for our happiness and our suffering. It is our own deeds.

Those who believe that everything is created by a creator can blame whom they may, even the deities. If you believe that a deity creates suffering and happiness, then, of course, that deity is to blame. However, though we may worship deities and pray to them, they do not help us when we are in a crisis.

For example, in South India, there is a small village with a typical village school. Since the village and the school are very poor, of course the roofs are all made of grass. One day there was a big fire. The roof burned very quickly, and soon the entire school was on fire. None of the small children were able to escape, and many of them died. Of course, their parents were terribly sad and they experienced great suffering. Their parents had been very religious. Every day, they did *pūjās* in their homes in front of statues of deities, and they made offerings and did traditional prayers. Their main prayer had always been, of course, for the safety of their children.

When the children died in the fire, the parents became so angry at their gods that they threw all of the statues into a ditch. If we believe that there are gods that create suffering, then of course we cannot blame the parents for discarding their statues. If we believe that the deities create all suffering and all happiness, then why would they give us suffering?

In the Buddhist tradition, we cannot lay blame at the feet of deities. The deities may help us in certain ways, but the main determinant is our own actions. It is due to our own bad deeds that we face suffering. It is also due to our own good deeds that we enjoy life. Because we have done virtuous deeds in the past, today we enjoy life. And because we have done nonvirtuous deeds in the past, today we suffer. Therefore, we cannot blame anybody else.

This is the Buddhist teaching of the law of cause and effect, or the law of karma. All good things in our lives—like a long life, good health, prosperity, and the fulfillment of our wishes—are due to the good deeds that we have performed in the past. Likewise, all bad things—such as short life, sickness, poverty, failures, and not being able to fulfill your wishes—are also due to our actions, the nonvirtuous deeds that we have committed in the past. Today we suffer from these deeds, so we cannot blame anybody else. We have to blame ourselves. This is the basic meaning of the law of karma. In order to practice the Dharma seriously, it is very important to think about this, and then to realize how important it is to practice the Dharma, to do so without wasting any time, and to do so effectively.

Among ordinary people, there are of course millions and millions who are not interested in any kind of spiritual path. There are many who are. Among these, there are some who *appear* to practice the Dharma but do not *really* practice the Dharma.

Even though we may recite prayers, wear robes, go to the temple, meditate, and so on, our mind can still be filled with worldly attachments and worldly thoughts. In this way, even apparent spiritual practice can be linked to worldly gain. Although these actions appear to be spiritual practices, in reality they are simply another worldly activity. In order to make our actions a true spiritual path, we should try not to think of worldly gains. We must try to embark on a true Dharma path that will lead to liberation and enlightenment. Even if we cannot do this perpetually, we can start by doing it for at least a few hours today.

This is why, in *Parting from the Four Attachments*, it says, "If you have attachment to this life, you are not a religious person." Actually, in Tibetan, the word *religious* means "dharmic." This point is very important. If we practice the Dharma but we do not do it the right way, the practice becomes just another worldly activity and is not a true Dharma practice.

The foundation of practice depends on what we call *ngöndro,* which means "preliminary practice." This is very important because through ngöndro, or foundation practices, we establish the basis of our path, our religious practice, our spiritual practice—genuine Dharma that will lead to liberation and enlightenment.

Nowadays many people think that ngöndro practice is just about counting refuge prayers, mantras, maṇḍala offerings, and things like that until you reach a certain number. And then, if you reach this number, you expect something to happen automatically. But unless these practices actually change your mind, then no matter how many mantras you recite or how many maṇḍala offerings you make, it will not make a real difference. It is when you are truly changing your mind that your practice is very good, even if you are only reciting a few mantras.

As mentioned above, reflection on the suffering of saṃsāra, the difficulty of obtaining a precious human life, impermanence, and the law of karma are very important. These are not something that you count or recite. Rather, you have to think about them in everyday life, while you are working, when you are around other people, when you are in the midst of your busy life. You can reflect on these at any time. You can think of saṃsāra, and you can think of suffering, and you can think of impermanence. You do not have to do this in a temple or in your shrine room or the like. Even while you are working or while you are traveling, you can think about these things, and doing this will lead your mind to the spiritual path.

So far, I have tried to describe these practices in common language and to say in plain words what the preliminary practices really mean. More formally, we can explain the preliminary practices by dividing them into common and uncommon preliminary practices. Some preliminary practices are common to all the Mahāyāna paths, whether Sūtrayāna or Mantrayāna, and so these are called "the common preliminaries." In addition to these, there are foundational practices primarily practiced in the Mantrayāna, also known as the Vajrayāna. These are called "the uncommon preliminaries."

The first practice of the uncommon preliminaries is taking refuge. It is also part of the common practices. Refuge has many different levels. The two main levels are worldly refuge and beyond-worldly refuge.

Worldly refuge itself has two types: object worldly refuge and mental worldly refuge. Object worldly refuge occurs when people face a crisis in life, a desperate situation, and they take refuge in spirits and local deities, or trees, mountains, rocks, and the like. Mental worldly refuge occurs when we take refuge in the right object, such as the Buddha, Dharma, and Saṅgha, but the purpose of doing so is only to have a long life, good health, prosperity, success, and to fulfill our wishes. Although the Triple Gem is the right object, the main purpose is still a worldly one. Neither worldly refuge is the right refuge.

Beyond-worldly refuge also has two types, that of the Hīnayāna, or Lesser Vehicle, and that of the Mahāyāna, or Greater Vehicle. (The Hīnayāna can, in turn, be divided into the vehicles of the śrāvakas and the pratyekabuddhas.)

Thus there are four major refuge paths in total, each with its own cause, object, duration, and purpose. These factors are what separate worldly from nonworldly refuge.

The main cause of worldly refuge is fear. Fear arises when we have some crisis in life, and due to this fear, we take refuge. The duration of this refuge is only as long as it takes to overcome the temporary problems or sufferings, and the purpose is just for our own sake.

In the Hīnayāna refuge, the main objective of the śrāvaka and the pratyekabuddha is not to become a buddha but to become an arhat. Śrāvakas take refuge mainly in the Saṅgha, and pratyekabuddhas take refuge mainly in the Dharma. These are the two types of Hīnayāna refuge.

Next, Mahāyāna refuge has three main causes. Generally the causes of taking refuge are fear, faith, and compassion. All three of these causes are present in the Mahāyāna refuge, but the most important one is compassion. In the Mahāyāna, every practice that we do is not for the sake of ourselves but for the sake of all sentient beings. To have this goal, it is necessary to have compassion. If you do not have compassion, how can you have a mind to help sentient beings? Thus the main cause of Mahāyāna refuge is compassion.

The object of refuge, as in all Buddhist traditions, is the Buddha, Dharma, and Saṅgha, but the Mahāyāna explanation is different. In the Mahāyāna tradition, the Buddha refers to one who possesses the three kāyas or bodies: the dharmakāya, the saṃbhogakāya, and the nirmāṇakāya.

Dharmakāya means the "body of reality." The dharmakāya is not something that we gain from the outside when the obscurations are cleared away. The dharmakāya is something that we already have and are unable to see because of the obscurations. Due to the natural purity that we all have, the true nature of the mind is pure and never stained with obscurations. If the true nature of the mind were itself stained with obscurations, then we would never be able to become free from them. But we can become free, because the obscurations are only temporary and not part of the nature of the mind itself. We all possess this natural purity. But we do not see it, because at the moment we have the obscurations. The buddhas, through their accumulations of merit and wisdom, have cleared away all of the obscurations including their propensities. Thus, the dharmakāya of the buddhas is said to be "doubly pure."

Saṃbhogakāya means "body of enjoyment." When all obscurations are cleared away, great qualities are attained. We do not have these qualities at the moment, but when obscurations are cleared, you gain great powers. The ordinary physical body becomes the Buddha's body with thirty-two signs and eighty qualities. The ordinary voice becomes the voice of the melody of Brahma, with the sixty branches. The ordinary mind becomes omniscient wisdom.

Nirmāṇakāya means "body of emanations." To explain them, the dharmakāya is invisible and beyond ordinary perception. The dharmakāya is ultimate reality, and it is only visible among buddhas. The saṃbhogakāya is visible to the highest level of the Buddha's followers like the bodhisattvas, but it is not visible to ordinary beings. However, the nirmāṇakāya, or emanation body, is revealed wherever, whenever, in whatever form the situation requires. It may be a human form or an animal's form—all kinds of different forms can appear to help beings.

The Buddha as one who possesses the three kāyas is described only in the Mahāyāna. Next, the term *Dharma* encompasses two meanings: the Buddha's teachings and realizations. The realizations are what buddhas and bodhisattvas have gained by eliminating all obscurations and thus fulfilling the truth of cessation and the truth of the path. This explanation of the Dharma is also specific to the Mahāyāna. Finally, the term *Saṅgha* actually means "community." In the context of the Mahāyāna refuge, the term refers to the holy community, the true Saṅgha—namely, the bodhisattvas who have already reached the irreversible state. In this way the Buddha, Dharma, and Saṅgha are the objects of refuge. The Mahāyāna's special refuge is with these objects.

Then we come to the duration of refuge: since our goal is to accomplish ultimate enlightenment for the sake of all sentient beings, we take refuge until enlightenment is reached. For example, if you want to go to an unknown place, the first thing you need is a guide who can show you the path. In this way, the Buddha is our guide. We need to rely on the guide until we reach our destination, and in this case, our destination is to accomplish ultimate enlightenment. Therefore, until enlightenment is reached, we take refuge in the Buddha. To reach your destination, you need to actually travel on the path—by walking, by car, or by other means. Similarly, we take refuge in the Dharma as our actual path. When one takes such a long and difficult journey, having trusted companions is very helpful. And therefore, we take refuge in the Saṅgha as our companions.

The purpose of Mahāyāna refuge is not for one's own sake but for the sake of all sentient beings. Because we believe in a cycle of rebirth, it follows that all sentient beings have been our mother and our very dear ones in previous lives. We are born into different families, take different forms, and lead different lives, but at one time or another, everyone—every sentient being—has been our parent, our very dear friend, and so on. Due to the change of life, we do not recognize each other and we see some people as friends, some as enemies, and toward some we are indifferent when, in reality, everyone is the same. Everyone is everyone's mother.

It is not proper to now ignore all of our mother sentient beings and seek liberation or enlightenment only for ourselves. Even on the worldly level, imagine that your closest family members, dearest ones, friends, or other relatives are in great suffering while you yourself are in a safe and happy place. If you are a good-hearted person, you would not feel happy in such circumstances. Even if you were unable to help them, you would at least try to do something to share their miseries. Similarly, all sentient beings are our mothers. All sentient beings have been our very dear ones. Ignoring them and just seeking liberation or enlightenment for oneself alone is not right.

Instead, we seek enlightenment for the sake of all sentient beings. The main purpose of taking refuge is not for your own benefit, your own way of being, but for the well-being of all sentient beings. This focus is what makes the Mahāyāna refuge special in terms of the cause, object, duration, and purpose of refuge.

Taking refuge is the very first of the preliminary practices. Of course, those who are followers of the Vajrayāna path also need to take Vajrayāna refuge, which a teacher can only give when you receive a major empowerment. It is also important that one create enlightenment mind. Refuge and enlightenment mind go together because, as I said, the main purpose is to help sentient beings.

To enter the spiritual path, and to succeed in attaining full enlightenment, we have to overcome our many obscurations. We have many negative deeds that we have accumulated throughout many lifetimes, and these have to be purified. The best way to purify them is through the practice of the Vajrayāna path, through Vajrasattva meditation and the recitation of Vajrasattva's one-hundred-syllable mantra.

At the same time, we need to accumulate merit, and there are many ways to do this. The most effective way is to make maṇḍala offerings. All of these are, of course, Vajrayāna practices, and one can only do them after receiving a major empowerment.

To receive blessings quickly, another crucial practice is guru yoga. In order to attain enlightenment, you need to realize the nature of the mind. The nature of the mind cannot be realized by explanation or by giving examples or by giving logical reasoning. It can only be realized through the accumulation of merit and through receiving the blessings of the guru. Therefore, guru yoga is very important. In this way you should emphasize the preliminary practices.

3. The Value of Retreat

THE PURPOSE OF RECEIVING teachings and empowerments is to practice them. If you do not cultivate the teachings and empowerments through practice, but only hear them and learn about them, then this will not fulfill your wish. Once you receive teachings, you must practice them. You can actually practice them anywhere, including in your own home. However, for a beginner, this can be difficult. The world has many distractions, and we live such busy lives with our families, commitments, and so on. This is why it becomes important to perform retreats.

When you do a retreat, you are removed from the distracting world, in a secluded place with no noise and no worldly activity, so that your mind can be focused and calm. In this situation, the practices that you do—recitations, meditations, and visualizations—will be much more effective. Once you have done a retreat and it is effective, once you have built a sound base, then you can continue your practice anywhere on a daily basis. This is why doing a retreat is very important. It is also important to do it *soon*, for as the Buddha said, everything is impermanent. In particular, our human life has no definite span. Anything can happen, but one thing that is one hundred percent certain is this: everyone who is born in this universe is going to die. There is no doubt about this whatsoever. Death will come sooner or later, and nobody can determine when it will come. Many people think, "I am young, I have time, and I am healthy, so at the moment I'll just enjoy the world and then later I will practice." This is totally wrong. Whether you will really have such a chance or not is very difficult to say. Therefore, it is very important to undertake serious practice right away.

It is possible to do a retreat on your own, but as individuals, this is difficult. You need a conducive place, you need a retreat manual text, you need offerings to set up, and you need instructions, etc. For all these conditions to come together is difficult and very rare. But in an organized retreat, we try our best to create these conditions so that retreat participants will not have problems with their shrines or setting up their offerings—so that they will have an appropriate place and the texts that they require, and so that the right rituals can be performed. In the beginning, your instructor will give the teachings so that you will possess full knowledge. During the retreat, from time to time, someone will give supplementary instructions. At the end of the retreat, when you are required to perform fire pūjās and the like, the retreat organizers will arrange it so that you will not need to worry about everything by yourself. For individuals on their own to try to get this text from here and that text from somewhere else can be very difficult.

Teachings, especially the Lamdré, have been given in many places, so now there are many people in many places who have received the full teachings and empowerments and who need to practice them. As I said, the purpose of receiving the Lamdré is to practice it. This is the reason we organize retreats.

Some people are concerned that retreat means that you are renouncing the world, and the Mahāyāna way emphasizes the commitment to help sentient beings. Indeed, it is true that every Mahāyāna practice is not for your own sake but for the sake of all other sentient beings, and it is important to engage in activities that help sentient beings. But at the moment we are ordinary people. We do not have the ability to really help all sentient beings. We do not have the knowledge and we do not have full power to help all beings, so first we have to cultivate within ourselves the power and ability to help.

Therefore, you need to do a retreat. You cannot do this simply by practicing a few sādhanas here and there in your busy world full of distractions. But if you do a retreat, even if it is only for a few months, then you will have a good foundation. The best retreat is one that is based on experiencing certain signs and realizations. But if you cannot do a sign retreat, then you can at least do a timed retreat or a number-of-mantras retreat. If you can do that, then you will have a foundation, some kind of power or strength that you can then use to help beings. Otherwise, without any abilities, how can you help other sentient beings? Therefore, doing retreat is very important for your own sake as well as the sake of others.

As it says in the tantras and also in the commentaries, retreat means that you are completely away from the busy world. There should be outer boundaries, inner boundaries, and innermost boundaries. You do not go out, and only certain people are allowed to come in. Other than these individuals, there is absolutely no link between the outside world and yourself.

Physically, you should not be seen and you should not see other people. If you see other people, this is called "making holes," because such contact punctures the boundaries of the retreat. And if other people see you, this is called "tearing," because such incidents mar the retreat. Even if you do see outsiders, they should not hear your voice, and, ideally, seeing them should not disturb your mind, either. That is difficult, but you should try to concentrate on your practice as much as possible.

Up until now, we have done a number of organized teachings, but so far we have not done many organized retreats in our tradition. Therefore, to benefit people all over the world who have received the teachings, especially the Lamdré teaching, we are now organizing retreat programs.

Part Two

The Sakya Tradition

4. Basic Teachings

The Buddha's Teachings

The great Lord Buddha resolved to attain enlightenment for the benefit of all sentient beings without exception. His primary goal was to achieve enlightenment and remove all sentient beings from the suffering of saṃsāra. Thus he created the enlightenment thought (*bodhicitta*): the wish to attain enlightenment for the sake of all sentient beings. After that, he accumulated enormous amounts of wisdom and compassion and finally attained perfect enlightenment, at which point he left behind all obscurations and attained every possible good quality. After attaining enlightenment, he performed many great activities—physical activities, verbal activities, and mental activities. Among all of these great activities, the most important activities were verbal—namely, the turning of the wheel of Dharma. Through the turning of the wheel of Dharma, the Buddha taught what he realized to sentient beings so that we, too, can be led to the path, proceed along it, and gain liberation and enlightenment ourselves.

But sentient beings are limitless. Since space itself has no limit, sentient beings have no limit. All sentient beings have different minds, mentalities, propensities, tastes, and so forth. So in order to suit every condition and mentality, the Buddha gave an enormous number of teachings. Like a skillful physician who uses many different medicines to cure many different diseases, the Buddha gave many different teachings in order to help sentient beings at different levels.

The Buddha has many types of teachings, which we can summarize and divide into various categories. Categorized in terms of the time they were given, there are three "turnings of the wheel of Dharma"—with the first turning of the wheel of Dharma also known as the first Dharmacakra, the second turning as the second Dharmacakra, and the third turning as the third Dharmacakra. Categorized in terms of subject, the collection of the Buddha's teachings is known as the Tripiṭaka, which consists of the Abhidharma, the Vinaya (the rules by which monks and nuns abide), and the Sūtras.

The whole purpose of turning the wheel of Dharma is to tame our mind, which is sullied by three main defilements. As the antidote for desire, the Buddha taught the Vinaya, which explains how to maintain and discipline our moral conduct. As the antidote for hatred, he taught the Sūtras, which explain all the different meditations that control and calm our mind. And the antidote for ignorance is the Abhidharma, which explains wisdom.

Additionally, there are two types of followers of the Buddhist Way: those who strive to attain the smaller goal of enlightenment for themselves and those who strive to attain the greater goal of enlightenment for all. Based on the differing goals, the Buddha's teachings can be categorized with two main vehicles: the Hīnayāna, or Lesser Vehicle, which aims for the smaller goal, and the Mahāyāna, or Greater Vehicle, which aims for the greater goal.

Tibetan Buddhism

Although Buddhism started in India and then went to many countries, only Tibet has all the teaching levels—the Hīnayāna, Mahāyāna, and Vajrayāna—as well as other related teachings. Practitioners in Tibet are all Mahāyāna Buddhists. Mahāyāna can be divided into two parts, the cause yāna and the result yāna. General Mahāyāna is called "cause yāna" because it takes a long time to work on the cause, and thus it takes a long time to achieve results. Mantrayāna, or Vajrayāna, is called the "result yāna" because it is easier to achieve results and the result emerges right from the beginning; the results can be taken into the path.

All of the different schools of Tibetan Buddhism are Mahāyāna combined with Vajrayāna methods and techniques. Thus, the major schools of Tibetan Buddhism are all similar; there is no substantial difference between them from the first development of enlightenment thought up to the final attainment of enlightenment. There is only one noteworthy difference: the lineage. Different lineages formed based on where the teaching started in India. The lineages then came to Tibet through various translators and then down through various masters and have continued to this day. Since each lineage is different, the emphasis of each is somewhat different. Some schools emphasize study, others emphasize meditation, and so on. But among the major schools of Tibetan Buddhism, the goal and motivation from the beginning to the end of the path is the same.

5. The Sakya Lineage in Historical Context

BUDDHISM CAME TO TIBET from India in two different periods. The first was during the eighth century in the time of the great abbot Śāntarakṣita, the great Guru Padmasambhava, and the Tibetan Dharma kings. Although during the time of Songtsen Gampo in the seventh century, some teachings and practices were introduced, there were no complete Buddhist teachings. It was during the time of Śāntarakṣita, Guru Padmasambhava, and King Trisong Deutsen that real Buddhism formed in Tibet. This is the time when the monastic traditions were established.

When Śāntarakṣita was attempting to establish a monastic tradition and building temples, there were many disturbances caused by local Tibetan guardians or spirits. Śāntarakṣita would build temples during the day, and at night the work would be destroyed. Śāntarakṣita then suggested that Guru Padmasambhava be invited. Guru Padmasambhava came, and he subdued the evil spirits and made the remaining ones become Buddhist protectors. Once this was accomplished, the trouble subsided, and the work of establishing the Dharma proceeded very smoothly. These were the great blessings of Guru Padmasambhava at the very beginning. In this period, the collection of the Buddha's teachings known as the *Kangyur* and the collection of the great commentaries known as the *Tengyur* were translated into Tibetan. With this, authentic Buddhism was established.

The Sakya tradition was established by and flourished within the Khön family. The Khön are believed to be direct descendants of celestial beings who originally came down to dwell on the high mountains of Tibet. Some of them returned, but others stayed, and the family line descended from those who stayed. At that time, they were known as the "Clear Light Celestial Race." This was the original name for the Khön family. In this early period, outwardly, the Khön were engaged in a struggle with the *rakṣās,* or demons. These rakṣās were defeated. Inwardly, these early Khön were emanations of Mañjuśrī. Thus, inwardly, Mañjuśrī defeated ignorance. The word *Khön* originates from this. *Khön* means disagreement—disagreement outwardly with the rakṣās and inwardly with ignorance.

A second name of the Sakya is "Pure Khön." In the time of the original Khöns, which was very long ago, there was not yet writing and thus no literature exists that describes their lives or activities. However, we know that at that time there was only the Bön religion in Tibet, and that the Khöns were originally Bön practitioners.

When Śāntarakṣita and Guru Padmasambhava brought Buddhism to Tibet in the eighth century, the Khön became involved in Buddhism. The first Buddhist Khön was named Khön Nāgendrarakṣita, and he was a great translator. During this period, Tibetans began to receive full Buddhist monastic ordination for the first time. Because there were doubts about whether Tibetans would be able to keep the vows, only seven individuals were chosen for a kind of trial: three young people, three old people, and one middle-aged person. Khön Nāgendrarakṣita was one of the three young ones. They all received the full Buddhist *bhikṣu* ordination from Śāntarakṣita, and they were all very successful in keeping the vinaya. This was the auspicious beginning of the great Tibetan Buddhist monastic tradition. Later, of course, thousands and thousands of monasteries were established with hundreds of thousands of monks and nuns.

Khön Nāgendrarakṣita had a younger brother known as Rinchen Dorjé. Rinchen Dorjé was a householder, not a monk. Both Khön Nāgendrarakṣita and Rinchen Dorjé received many empowerments and teachings, including Vajrakīlaya and Samyak Heruka, and these became the main deities of the Khön tradition. For many generations, the Khöns practiced these two deities and accomplished great realizations and great miracles. This continued for a very long time during which the Khön family were Nyingmapas, or followers of the tradition of the earlier translations.

A Tibetan king named Langdarma destroyed many Buddhist teachings and practices, and this caused a gap in the flourishing of Buddhism in Tibet. After that, the Buddhadharma began to spread again and was again brought from India. This second period is called the "new translation," or *sarma*, period. The new translation schools are the Sakya, Kagyü, and Geluk traditions.

The Khön family switched from Nyingma and established the Sakya because, after many generations, they felt that auspicious conditions were ripening for the establishment of a separate school. To this end, during the eleventh century, during Khön Könchok Gyalpo's time, they attempted to conceal the ancient or Nyingma teachings. However, signs arose that the protectors of Vajrakīlaya and Heruka were displeased, and they found that they could not conceal the Vajrakīlaya cycle of teachings. This is why, although we are now a new tradition, from the old tradition we still carry on the Vajrakīlaya teaching and consider Vajrakīlaya to be one of our principal deities and one of our main practices, right up to the present day.

Khön Könchok Gyalpo had an older brother who said to him, "I am old now and unable to learn. But you are younger, and you must learn from the new tradition." When Khön Könchok Gyalpo heard about Drokmi Lotsāwa, the most famous living master in Tibet at that time, he went to him to request teachings. Drokmi Lotsāwa's full name is Drokmi Lotsāwa Shākya Yeshé. *Lotsāwa* means translator. From Drokmi Lotsāwa, Khön Könchok Gyalpo received many teachings, in particular the Lamdré and Hevajra cycle of teachings. Later, Khön Könchok Gyalpo's son, Sachen Künga Nyingpo, received the full cycle of Lamdré teachings from the disciples of Drokmi Lotsāwa's disciples, and so on.

The Sakyapas are called the lineage holders of the four great Tibetan translators. These four are Bari Lotsāwa (also known as Rinchen Drak), Drokmi Lotsāwa Shākya Yeshé, Mal Lotsāwa Lodrö Drakpa, and Lotsāwa Rinchen Sangpo. The teachings, pith instructions, and traditions that were brought to Tibet by these four translators were practiced and disseminated by the Sakya order. The teachings that came from these translators were considered to be very authentic because the translators went all the way to India from Tibet, where they met great Indian masters and studied for a long time, bringing the teachings with them back to Tibet. As such, these teachings are held to be very authentic and very pure, and so they have been kept and transmitted.

Generally speaking, all of the schools of Tibetan Buddhism are the same in agreeing that the most important thing is motivation. Whatever practice we do, whatever teachings we receive, the place where the practice eventually leads depends upon our motivation. The motivation in all of the Tibetan Buddhist schools is the same; every school wishes to attain enlightenment for the sake of all sentient beings. In this there is absolutely no difference between schools.

Regarding the main practice, all schools emphasize both method and wisdom. Method is also called "means." It includes such practices as generosity, moral conduct, patience, meditation, etc. These are similar in all the schools. Wisdom means finding the ultimate truth, or knowing the ultimate nature of all phenomena. Regarding wisdom, every Tibetan Buddhist school follows what is called the Madhyamaka, or the Middle Way.

Ordinary people do not bother to inquire about the true nature of things or ask what reality is. They just take life as it is. But more intelligent people try to find out about the nature of reality. What we see and what reality is are two different things. For example, people who have certain diseases like jaundice will see the moon as yellow in color because of their sickness. What we apprehend—like form, sound, smell, taste, etc.—is not the ultimate truth of these phenomena.

What then is the ultimate nature or truth of phenomena?

There are different answers to this question. Non-Buddhist schools have answers that differ from Buddhist schools. There are different answers, too, among the different philosophical schools in Buddhism. The highest, which is known as the Buddha's most important teaching, is called the perfection of wisdom, or *prajñāpāramitā*. Later, this was explained by the great Indian master Nāgārjuna.

The Buddha himself prophesied that four hundred years after his mahāparinirvāṇa, there would be a bhikṣu named Nāga who would be able to explain the true meaning of the *prajñāpāramitā*. As the Buddha prophesied, Nāgārjuna came into the world and explained the philosophy of Madhyamaka, or the Middle Way. Madhyamaka differs from other schools in that the Middle Way school offers no conclusion as such. All of the other schools have a conclusion: it is like this, or it is like that.

In the Madhyamaka, all phenomena are explained in two ways, in terms of relative truth and absolute truth. Relative truth takes what ordinary people see just as it is. We accept that there is form to see, that there is sound to hear, that there are smells, tastes, and so on. However, when we try to find the absolute truth, there can be no conclusion. This is because the absolute truth is away from all explanation, perceptions, descriptions, and words. You cannot describe it as being this way or that way. It is beyond words, perceptions, and explanations.

Since the basic motivation and the main practice of all schools of Tibetan Buddhism are the same, the final accomplishment of enlightenment is also the same. All Tibetan Buddhists are absolutely not different from one another, except that the lineages of all four schools are different; they differ with respect to the lineage of masters by which the teachings have been passed down. Their original Indian gurus may be different, the translators were different, how the teachings were brought from India and passed down from one master to the next are different. The emphasis of each school is somewhat different. Some schools emphasize studies, while others put more emphasis on meditation. But other than these things, there is really no difference at all between the Tibetan Buddhist schools.

As mentioned earlier, because all beings are different, it is necessary for there to be a variety of practices. For example, there are hundreds and thousands of deities. But all of the deities are actually the ultimate transcendental wisdom of the Buddha. The omniscient Buddha is the same, and there is no difference between the deities. For the sake of practitioners and followers, however, they appear to be different. As such, some deities are wrathful, some are peaceful, some have very elaborate forms with many hands, heads, and legs, while others are very simple, with one face and two hands. Some are surrounded by hundreds of other deities; some appear alone or in very simple form. All of this is due to the fact that we have different interests. Some people are inclined toward wrathful deities. Some are inclined toward peaceful deities. Some prefer elaborate forms, and some prefer simple forms. Some are intrigued by deities surrounded by many thousands of other deities, and some are attracted to a solitary deity. But of course all of the practices are really the same.

The Sakyapas have historical connections with all of the Tibetan Buddhist schools. The Khöns were originally Nyingmapas. They were direct disciples of the Guru Padmasambhava, and their main practices were Vajrakīlaya and Samyak Heruka. The Nyingma, then, is like our grandfather; it is where we came from originally. Next, the Kagyüpas and the Sakyapas are like twin brothers. These two lineages were founded around the same time, and they share the same practices. One of the main practices of the Kagyü tradition is Hevajra, the main practice of the Sakya tradition. The founder of the Kagyü tradition, Lhodrak Marpa Chökyi Lodrö (Marpa Lotsāwa) went to India and brought back many teachings, including the Hevajra cycle. The *Hevajra Tantra* taught in the two schools is similar. There are two translations of the *Hevajra Tantra* in Tibetan. One was translated by Drokmi Lotsāwa Shākya Yeshé, and the other was translated by the Marpa Lotsāwa Chökyi Lodrö. The translations are similar, and the teachings are the same.

The practicing philosophy of these two schools is similar, too. In the Sakyapa tradition, the master of the highest importance after the five founders is Ngorchen Dorjé Chang Künga Sangpo, who founded the Ngor sect, a kind of subschool of the Sakya tradition. Ngorchen Künga Sangpo wrote many commentaries on many tantras, and especially on the Hevajra cycle of teachings. In his commentaries, he clearly illustrated the various traditions and their respective practices of the Hevajra cycle. These exist because in India there were different Buddhist traditions practicing Hevajra. After studying all of the Hevajra teachings from the various traditions from India, he rejected and refuted some of them. He then continued with additional study and repeated contemplation and found that the teachings that came from Marpa Lotsāwa in the Kagyü tradition were similar to the Sakya traditions.

Another great Sakyapa master is Ngorchen Künga Sangpo's disciple, Gorampa Sönam Sengé, who wrote many commentaries on the sūtras as well as on the tantras. Today, the philosophical studies in all of our Sakya monasteries, and especially in the colleges, include study of a text written by Gorampa Sönam Sengé. This work is called *Distinguishing the Different Philosophical Views*, and it describes the views and practices of many different schools. Gorampa states in this work that the followers of the true Madhyamaka philosophy were the ancient translators, the great Sakyapa masters, and Milarepa. All those who follow the Madhyamaka hold the same view, and view is the essence of our practice. Of course, rituals with chanting and music are slightly different in every monastery.

But this aspect is not really important. If all of the schools share a similar view, then what other similarity is needed?

Next we have the Gelukpas, founded by Lama Tsongkhapa. Lama Tsongkhapa did most of his sūtric studies in the Sakya Monastery. His main teacher for many years was Rendawa Shönnu Lodrö, one of the assistant abbots of Sakya. Lama Tsongkhapa received his Vajrayāna teachings and empowerments from Lama Dampa Sönam Gyaltsen, who was one of the throneholders of the Sakya tradition. In this way, the Gelukpa is like our nephew. As you can see, all of the three traditions are very much connected; the differences between the Tibetan schools are mainly a matter of the lineages in which the teachings were passed down.

Later on, three great masters—Jamyang Khyentsé Wangpo, Tertön Chokgyur Lingpa, and Jamgön Kongtrül Lodrö Thayé—followed what is called the nonsectarian tradition. These masters received teachings from every school, and they combined them and practiced them all. They also wrote commentaries and compiled the great treasuries or collections of sādhanas and collections of tantras, containing empowerments, initiations, blessings, and teachings from all the different schools of Tibetan Buddhism. In fact, even the lineages are very much connected together. In the many collections of sādhanas from the Nyingma, Sakya, Kagyü, Geluk, and other schools, all masters of the teaching lineages are assembled together and can be seen to be essentially the same.

Further, there is no difference between the deities in terms of their wisdom, compassion, or power. It is due to our karmic affinity that certain deities are easier to accomplish and others are more difficult to accomplish. This is why it is important to find a deity appropriate to one's own karmic connections. Similarly, we can have karmic connections with different schools. Some people are karmically connected with the Sakya, some with the Kagyü, some with the Geluk or Nyingma, and so on. Whatever school is your karmic connection should be taken as your main practice.

We must also regard all of the schools with the right view and with pure vision. This means that we should see each school as the actual activity of the Buddha himself, having established different schools with different purposes. In this way, one can earn great merit and receive great blessings from every school. In the past, there were times where sectarian activities occurred. In recent times, due to the great blessings and guidance of His Holiness the Dalai Lama, Tibetan Buddhism has been brought into a harmonious unity, with pure vision for all schools. Thanks to this, everyone benefits and receives blessings and can enrich their practices. In Vajrayāna practice, pure practice or commitment (*samaya*) is very important. If samaya is not pure, then it is very difficult to gain experience and realization. But if you have pure samaya, then it is easy to achieve realization and experience.

It is very important to understand these things. I attempted here to give a brief overview of the Sakyapa lineage practice, which has traditionally been carried down from the Khön lineage up to this very day.

Looking to the Future

In 2014, when I came to the United States of America, I thought that it was necessary to make some changes in the way in which the future heads of the order are selected. At the moment, we were completely united. But if the status quo remained unchanged, problems might arise in the future. It was therefore necessary for us to make some changes in our system in the Sakya tradition.

The proposed change was not really an essential change. In our tradition, of course, the Khön lineage holders are recognized as the head of the Sakya order. Everyone recognizes that this system is historically established. However, while I was in the United States of America, I made a visit to Seattle and held a discussion with members of the Phuntsok Phodrang branch of the Sakya order, in particular with Dagchen Rinpoche, the head of Phuntsok Phodrang. Since we two were the senior members of the Sakya school, we felt that while we are still alive it should be our responsibility to help the younger generation in our tradition so that there will not be confusion or problems when they succeed to the leadership of the Sakya school. After the discussion, the Phuntsok Phodrang members were in complete agreement with what was proposed. The agreement was written down, read, signed, and sealed at that time. However, the proposal was not immediately announced. I had an audience with His Holiness the Dalai

Lama, in which I presented His Holiness with the signed agreement and sought his blessings and suggestions.

His Holiness the Dalai Lama was very pleased with the proposal and remarked that this was the best news. Thus, His Holiness gave his full blessing and his permission, together with an acknowledgment letter.

Traditionally, the leadership of the Sakya school rotated between the two palaces, the Phuntsok Phodrang, who currently lives in Seattle, and our Dolma Phodrang. The two palaces in fact have the same father and mother if we trace back many previous generations. The founders of the palaces were actually brothers, and the heads of the two palaces have been taking turns as the head of the Sakya tradition, and this position has usually been based on seniority. The appointment was for life. As such, the younger members of the Khön family had almost no chance to become head. Because of these problems, we felt it was necessary for us to propose a change in this system.

There is a further reason to support this proposal. A long time ago, when I was still young and living in Tibet, one of the greatest masters in Tibet, one of my gurus, the great Vajradhara Jamyang Khyentsé Chökyi Lodrö, suggested that members of the two palaces could take turns as head of the Sakya school for a three-year term. This would be similar to the headship of the Ngor palaces, the subsect of the Sakya school. In the Ngor tradition, there are four palaces, and the head of each palace takes a turn to be appointed as the head of Ngor tradition every three years. Jamyang Khyentsé Chökyi Lodrö proposed that the Dolma and Phuntsok palaces adopt such a system in order to avoid confusion and problems in the system. It was impossible to implement this at that time in Tibet, but I think that now is a good time for us to begin. Khyentsé Dorjé Chang was a great master, and his suggestions certainly carry great blessings. I brought this up to Dagchen Rinpoche, and apparently Dagchen Rinpoche also recalled this. He verified that, indeed, Khyentsé Dorjé Chang did make these suggestions.

In the new system, every Khön family member who meets the qualifications stated in the document would be eligible to be chosen to be the head of the Sakya order, and in this way, everyone would have an opportunity to be the head. There are only two palaces officially, but in reality, every *dungsei* (son of a Khön-family lineage holder) has his own family and they stay in different houses. Strictly speaking, then, there are more than two palaces. In the new system, everyone from each palace would have a chance to lead the Sakya school. Many people think this will be a big change. But in reality, it will not be a real change. It is still the same tradition, and the Sakya tradition will still be led by Khön members. The only difference is that the duration of the appointment is being altered, providing an opportunity for every Khön member who is qualified to have an equal chance to become the head of the order.

The official announcement of the new system was made at the Mönlam in 2014. According to the Tibetan astrological chart, 2016 was going to be an inauspicious year. But 2017 was believed to be a good year, and so we began implementing this new system in 2017, as stated in the signed agreement. Moreover, the new system had an additional advantage in that the dungseis from both palaces were already fully grown. Some had already completed their studies and others were finishing their studies. It was a good time for them to assume responsibility for leading the tradition because their elders were still alive. If they were to take leadership roles without us, it might be difficult for them when they want to seek advice and so on. While senior members are still alive, however, we can provide suggestions and direction when they encounter problems.

6. How the Lamdré Teaching Began

TODAY, THE SAKYA LINEAGE is the owner of many great and varied teachings in the Sūtra and Mantra Vehicles. But the most important teaching in our tradition is the Lamdré, which means "the path that includes the result." This teaching originated in India from the great mahāsiddha Virūpa, who was one of the eighty-four mahāsiddhas. Virūpa was born in a royal family and had special qualities from a very young age. He saw that everything in saṃsāra was suffering and so renounced it to become a monk. He entered the great monastery of Nālandā, where he first studied the Sūtrayāna teachings and later received the Mantrayāna teachings and practices. Virūpa became very famous, and later he became the abbot of Nālandā Monastery. He taught Mahāyāna teachings to hundreds and thousands of monks, held debate sessions, and composed many books on the general Mahāyāna. He also practiced the Mantrayāna in secret.

But after practicing for a long period of time, Virūpa did not experience significant signs of attainment. He felt that perhaps he did not have a karmic connection with tantric practice and so wanted to devote his time fully to the Mahāyāna teaching. But on the very night he made this decision, he saw in a vision the great ḍākinī Vajra Nairātmyā. She said, "What you have decided is wrong. I am your karmic-link deity. You must continue your Vajrayāna practices." After having this vision, he continued his Vajrayāna practice.

Shortly thereafter, Virūpa had another pure vision of the full maṇḍala of Vajrayoginī and received the empowerment of its special deity, Hevajra. Afterward he achieved great realizations every night for six nights. On the first night, he realized the first *bhūmi*, or stage of the bodhisattva path, realizing the ultimate truth. From the second night onward, he attained one bhūmi every night up to and including the sixth bhūmi, thereby becoming a great mahāsiddha. Virūpa then left the monastery and went on to perform many great miracles. He subdued many evils and corrected those on the wrong path. Many beings benefited just by hearing his name. He did a great service to the Buddhadharma.

The mahāsiddha Virūpa had many general Mahāyāna followers, but for the esoteric pith instructions, he had two main followers: Kṛṣṇācārya and Ḍombi Heruka. For Kṛṣṇācārya, Virūpa gave a teaching known as the Vajra Words. This very short teaching is the essence of all the Tripiṭaka and Vajrayāna; it is like butter churned from milk. This essence is the most important of all the Buddha's sūtras and tantras in the form of pith instructions.

This particular teaching was then passed from Kṛṣṇācārya to his disciple, and so on. Altogether, five Indian gurus received this teaching. The fifth Indian master was Gayādhara, who came to Tibet several times and gave this teaching to the great translator Drokmi Lotsāwa. Drokmi Lotsāwa was the first Tibetan to receive this particular Lamdré teaching. Drokmi Lotsāwa was very great and had many disciples. Many of them, both male and female, achieved great realizations.

Drokmi Lotsāwa gave the general tantric explanations and pith instructions separately. He would not give the tantric explanations to his disciples who had heard the pith instructions, because the tantric teachings were very precious. Consequently, none of his disciples were given both teachings at the same time.

Among Drokmi Lotsāwa's disciples, the most important was Setön Künrik, who received the Lamdré teachings and achieved high realization. Then Setön Künrik gave the teaching to Shangtön Chöbar, a "hidden yogi." To the general public, Shangtön Chöbar appeared as an ordinary person working in other people's fields, but inwardly, he was a great yogi. He promised to work in a variety of fields simultaneously and sent out emanations of his body enabling him to do so. He gave this Lamdré teaching to the great Lama Sakyapa (Sachen Künga Nyingpo), who was born in the Khön lineage.

The Khön lineage is said to directly descend from celestial beings. These celestial beings dwelt in a heavenly realm known as the *rūpadhātu*, or form realm, and when the time was ripe, they felt that it was necessary to descend to the human realm. Three brothers descended to the high mountains of Tibet. One of them settled in Tibet and his lineage continued. The first name of this lineage is the Clear Light Race. Then the celestial beings mixed with the rakṣās, or local spirits.

Later there was some outward disagreement between the rakṣā beings and the celestial beings, but inwardly it was a disagreement between perfect wisdom and ignorance. After that, the lineage became known as Khön, and both the name and the lineage have continued to the present day. Before Buddhism came to Tibet, the Khön lineage were Bön practitioners. When Guru Padmasambhava brought Buddhism to Tibet, Khön Nāgendrarakṣita became his direct disciple. Guru Padmasambhava gave many teachings to Khön Nāgendrarakṣita, and he was one of the first seven Tibetans to receive the full Buddhist monastic (bhikṣu) ordination.

The test of whether these seven Tibetans would be able to keep their bhikṣu monastic vows came out very successfully, and this marked the auspicious beginning of the monastic tradition in Tibet. After that, the entire Khön lineage became practitioners of the Nyingmapa tradition until the time of Khön Könchok Gyalpo. At that time, the Khön lineage felt it was necessary to start a separate school, so they concealed all the ancient teachings and started the Sakya order.

The Sakya Monastery was founded in 1073 by Khön Könchok Gyalpo, who was the father of the great Lama Sakyapa, Sachen Künga Nyingpo. At that time, Könchok Gyalpo was also a tantric disciple of Drokmi Lotsāwa. So Sachen Künga Nyingpo received the *Hevajra Tantra* directly from his father, Könchok Gyalpo, who was a direct disciple of Drokmi Lotsāwa. However, Sachen Künga Nyingpo did not receive the pith instructions from his father. Instead, he went to the great practitioner Shangtön Chöbar for pith instructions.

At first Shangtön Chöbar hesitated to bestow the pith instructions upon Sachen Künga Nyingpo. But later, when he found out that Sachen Künga

Nyingpo was his Dharma brother's son, he was more eager to give him the pith instructions. After doing so, Shangtön Chöbar said, "For eighteen years, you are not allowed to disclose any of these pith instructions—not even the name of the instructions—to anyone. But after eighteen years you may disclose them to anyone and you can even write them down. It will be up to you. You are now the owner of this teaching."

In reality, Sachen Künga Nyingpo was already a fully enlightened being. He was actually the emanation of Mañjuśrī and Avalokiteśvara, the manifestations of all the buddhas' wisdom and compassion together in one person. But in an ordinary person's view, he still possessed a human body and therefore had to follow the human way of life. Accordingly, for eighteen years, Sachen Künga Nyingpo did not mention even a word of Lamdré to anyone and thereby kept the teaching secret. During those eighteen years, the great Lama Sakyapa rehearsed the teachings only to himself.

At one point during that period he became very ill, and because at that time the Lamdré was only transmitted orally, and none of the texts were written down, he forgot them. Sachen Künga Nyingpo was very worried. His guru had already passed away and he felt that even if he went to India it might be hard to find a teacher, because tantric practice was done only in secret places in the high mountains and the great forests; it was not commonly taught. And so he prayed very intensely. Then he had a dream.

In Sachen Künga Nyingpo's dream, his guru, Shangtön Chöbar, came to give him the teaching again. After this dream, Künga Nyingpo remembered much of the teaching. Again he prayed, and finally in an exalted meditation, Shangtön Chöbar appeared to give Künga Nyingpo many teachings. As a result, he remembered most of the teaching he had forgotten.

One day Mahāsiddha Virūpa, who was the original founder of the Lamdré teaching and received this teaching directly from the deity, appeared on the huge mountain near Sakya. The great mountain was at his back and Mahāsiddha Virūpa's body covered the huge mountain and he said, "This earth belongs to me." He then gave again the full Lamdré teaching, as well as other related teachings, to the great Sachen Künga Nyingpo. This is how the great Lama Sakyapa Künga Nyingpo became the holder of all the Buddha's teachings. He gave all these teachings to his sons and many of his disciples, who have continued the lineage up to the present day. This is a very brief history of how the Lamdré teaching began.

7. An Introduction to the Triple Vision

THE LAMDRÉ TEACHING is profound and vast. It can be practiced in many ways. Those destined to follow the gradual path will begin with the Hīnayāna path and then continue with the Mahāyāna and Vajrayāna paths. Others may be able to follow the direct path due to their state of mind and karmic connections. For this reason, there are many different ways to present the teaching to disciples. For most people, we typically present the whole teaching in two parts: the preliminary part and the main part. The preliminary part is known as the Triple Vision. The main part is known as the Triple Tantra, which we will not cover here.

The Triple Vision has three parts: (1) the impure vision, (2) the vision of experience, and (3) the pure vision.

The Impure Vision

At the base are sentient beings. Because of our impure karma, defilements, and actions, we have the impure vision. The yogis who practice meditation and are practitioners of the path have the vision of experience. After working very hard on the path, you can achieve the final result of buddhahood, at which point inner qualities are manifest that cause them to perceive the pure vision.

In the Lamdré, as in all Buddhist traditions, the first step—the basic practice of all paths, the root of all the Dharma, the foundation of all the vows, and the difference between Buddhist practitioners and others—is taking refuge in the Buddha, Dharma, and Saṅgha. All the meditations in Lamdré are divided into three parts: (1) taking refuge and creating the enlightenment thought, (2) the main part, and (3) the conclusion, which is a dedication. Like all other schools, the refuge section is further divided into five parts: (1) cause, (2) object, (3) method, (4) benefit, and (5) the vows of refuge.

First, the causes of taking refuge are fear, faith, and compassion.

Second, the objects of refuge are the Buddha, Dharma, and Saṅgha. In the Mahāyāna school, "Buddha" refers to "one who possesses the three kāyas, or bodies: the dharmakāya, nirmāṇakāya, and saṃbhogakāya." The Dharma is the teaching and realization. The true Saṅgha is the bodhisattvas who have reached the irreversible state.

Third, the method of taking refuge is to hold the Buddha as our guide, the Dharma as our path, and the Saṅgha as our spiritual companions.

Fourth, the benefit of taking refuge is immense; as it is said in the sūtra: "If the merit we earn from taking refuge had a form, the whole universe would be too small to contain it." This means the merit from taking refuge is unfathomably immense.

Fifth, the rules of refuge contain both general rules and specific rules, which are fully explained after one receives the refuge vow.

Suffering

The explanation of the impure vision is given first in order to encourage renunciation. This relates to the first of the four noble truths: the truth of suffering. As described in an earlier chapter, there are three types of sufferings: (1) the suffering of suffering, (2) the suffering of change, and (3) the suffering of the conditional nature of all things.

The suffering of suffering is the obvious suffering we all have, such as physical pain and mental anxiety. The animal realm, the hungry ghost realm, and the hell realm have a lot of this type of suffering. The suffering of suffering also exists in the higher realms, although we normally think that the higher realms are a mixture of suffering and happiness. But in reality, the experience of suffering in the higher realms is merely different in degree than it is in the lower realms. We all experience the suffering of physical pain and mental anxiety.

Second is the suffering of change. Anything that is created by causes and conditions is impermanent. Anything that is impermanent is in a process of change; it is suffering if it is always changing. The entire world is changing. Outside, every year we have different seasons; inside, the young grow old, large families become small and small families become large, and so on. Phenomena are always changing.

The third kind of suffering is the conditional nature of all things. Feelings that we normally categorize as "happy" or "indifferent" exist only in relation to other feelings. But in reality there is no real happiness. Throughout saṃsāra as a whole, from top to bottom, there is no real happiness, although there are certain places with lesser rather than greater suffering. If poison is mixed with food, whether it is good food or bad food, it is harmful. Similarly, in saṃsāra as a whole, there is not a single place that is worthy of attachment.

In order to arouse renunciation thought, we need to think about the sufferings of the six realms in great detail. As mentioned in a previous chapter, according to the teachings the whole universe is divided into six realms. There are three lower realms (hell realm, hungry ghost realm, and animal realm) and three higher realms (human realm, demigod realm, and god realm). But in reality, none of these is a completely happy place worthy of attachment. In order to arouse a genuine inner urge to be free from suffering, the first preliminary practice is to concentrate on the different conditions and different levels of suffering.

Precious Human Rebirth

The second preliminary practice is to meditate on the difficulty of obtaining a precious human birth. Due to our karma and defilements, ordinary sentient beings like us have impure vision. Where did this impure vision come from? It came through our own actions.

The only way to be completely free from this realm of existence is to practice the holy Dharma. To practice the holy Dharma, we first have to attain a precious human birth. As we've discussed, it is very rare to attain human birth. From the causal point of view, in order to be born as a human being, you must have very strong virtuous deeds—especially moral conduct, which is supported by other good deeds such as generosity and sincere aspirations. The convergence of all these causes is very rare.

When we think of the world today, how many people actually practice the spiritual path? Even many of those who appear to be practicing the Dharma are only doing so superficially. Since the cause is very rare, the result is also very rare. Therefore, from the causal point of view, it is very rare to have human birth.

Also, from a sheer numerical point of view, we assume that people exist in great numbers. But while it is very easy to count the number of people living in one house for example, it may prove impossible to count the number of insects and other small beings living in the same dwelling. Human birth is also rare in the context of nature as a whole.

Furthermore, taking into account the entire range of human life on earth in general, it is rare to be born free from the unfavorable states; or even to be born during the time when a buddha has come into the world and while his teachings are a living tradition and the conditions are right to practice the Dharma. And then even if we are fortunate enough to be born during that time, it is rarer still to be born with a sound mind to receive the teachings.

We must think that human life is very precious, more precious than a wish-fulfilling jewel. A wish-fulfilling jewel is the most precious possession you can have; with it, all of your material requirements such as food, medicine, and clothes can be fulfilled. But a wish-fulfilling jewel cannot bestow higher rebirth, self-liberation, or enlightenment. However, through this precious human body, if we work hard, not only can we achieve higher rebirth and personal liberation but even ultimate enlightenment is possible.

Therefore, we must not only intellectually understand the preciousness of a human birth but also feel inwardly that it is very precious and rare. There is no greater loss than wasting this very precious opportunity. If we cannot utilize this precious body now, we do not know that such an opportunity will ever come again in the future. Therefore, it is very important for us to work toward enlightenment when we have all the right conditions and are free from all the unfavorable states.

Since everything is impermanent, we must understand that our precious human birth is impermanent also. The sūtras state that the best offering to the Buddha is the contemplation of impermanence. Thinking about impermanence will turn away attachments. It will speed up our practice and effort on the spiritual path. It is also a great antidote for suffering. And thinking about impermanence will eventually help us to realize ultimate truth.

In this way, we must be mindful that this human existence that we now enjoy has no definite lifespan. We all know that people can die anytime: even before they are born or when they are babies, or when their children are grown, and so forth. Moreover, even if you have a certain lifespan to live out, there is no guarantee that you will necessarily make it, as anything could happen. Therefore, not only is it important to practice the Dharma but it is very important to practice it quickly without wasting any time.

The Law of Cause and Effect

The third preliminary practice is to contemplate the law of cause and effect. This is one of the unique teachings Lord Buddha gave in order to show what we must do and what practices we must follow. Everything we see and experience, including our current quality of life, has been created by our own actions. The teaching on cause and effect has two parts: the illusory vision and the karmic vision.

First, I will explain the illusory vision. The way we view the world now is grounded in dualism; we view the subject and object separately. Yet in reality neither exists. They are only illusions, like a dream. When we are dreaming, the experience seems real. But when we wake up, there is not even a trace of what we experienced in our dreams. Our lives are also like a great illusory vision. When subject and object are viewed as separate, this is known as dualistic illusory vision. Every ordinary sentient being experiences the world we live in with this dualistic illusory vision.

Second, the karmic vision consists of the different experience each sentient being has based on his or her karma. For example, some beings have more or less suffering, and so on. The actions we perform are like shadows following us wherever we go. There are three kinds of actions: physical, verbal, and mental. There are virtuous, nonvirtuous, and indifferent actions. Nonvirtuous actions are those undertaken out of ignorance, desire, or hatred. There are ten nonvirtuous deeds. Performing an action is like planting a seed. In due course the seed will ripen and produce results. If the root of a tree is poisonous, whatever grows on the tree, such as flowers and leaves, is also poisonous. Similarly, any actions undertaken from desire, hatred, or ignorance will lead to suffering in this life as well as in future lives.

Virtuous deeds are those that arise without the defilements—without desire and without hatred and ignorance. Virtuous actions are undertaken from loving-kindness and compassion. For example, if the root of a tree is medicinal, anything that grows on that tree is also medicinal. Similarly, any virtuous deeds created without the defilements will create happiness in this life as well as in future lives.

Finally, there are actions that are neither virtuous nor nonvirtuous, such as walking and sitting. Since these actions do not produce any negative results, they are better than the nonvirtuous actions; but since they do not produce any positive results, they are inferior to virtuous deeds. It is important to turn indifferent deeds into positive deeds and to abstain from negative deeds.

If you wish to be free from suffering, you must abstain from negative deeds. Begin by abstaining from the cause; if you indulge in a negative cause, then you cannot expect to have happiness as the result. Therefore, abstain from even the tiniest negative deed, and try your best to practice even the smallest virtuous deeds. In the same way that an accumulation of drops of water forms a great ocean, even tiny virtuous deeds will gradually accumulate and produce a great beneficial result. Regarding indifferent actions that are neither virtuous nor nonvirtuous, you should change your motivation using the skillful means of following the bodhisattva's way of life. You should also try to purify negative deeds through diligent practice.

With this, I have briefly explained the impure vision, which is the first part of the teaching.

The Vision of Experience

The second part of the Triple Vision is the vision of experience, which has two parts: (1) the common vision of experience and (2) the uncommon vision of experience.

The common vision of experience is experienced by common yogis and Mahāyāna practitioners. These practitioners apply themselves to common meditations on loving-kindness, compassion, and bodhicitta. Through this they attain the vision of experience.

In order to arouse the vision of experience, first we must practice loving-kindness. To practice loving-kindness we need to really understand that saṃsāra is full of suffering and that nobody wants to suffer. Everybody wants to be free from suffering, and we must work to free them from suffering.

First we aspire to gain personal liberation and freedom, and ultimately nirvāṇa, for ourselves. However, this is only an intermediate goal; if we carefully consider the situation, we can see that this is not the ultimate goal. Working for oneself alone is not the highest aspiration. For example, could you stay comfortably in a safe place if the other members of your family were in great trouble? If you are a good and kind-hearted person, you would not be happy but would rather go and try to help the other members of your family.

In our tradition we believe that our present awareness is a continuum. Since our present body came from our parents' similar bodies, likewise, our awareness must have come from mind similar to what we experience now. From birth to old age, although our consciousness changes, that mental continuum remains the same. In this sense, there is no gap in the continuum—the same mind is simply taking different forms. This same example is used to prove that our mind must have existed before the formation of our physical body. Likewise, when we die, our mind will not be burned or buried but will continue on in another form.

In this sense, an individual mind is not considered to have a beginning. From beginningless time until now we have continued in this realm of existence. We have taken birth, we have died, and we have taken another body, but the mind remains a continuum. Because we have had countless previous births, we also believe that at one time or another, every sentient being has been our dear mother, father, relative, or friend. For that reason, abandoning other sentient beings in order to achieve our own salvation is not the proper goal of spiritual practice. We must continually work for the benefit of other sentient beings.

When we begin to consider developing loving-kindness, we should remember that every sentient being, even the most fearsome animal, has an instinctive capacity for loving-kindness. Even fearsome lions tenderly love their cubs. We all have a certain level of loving-kindness, but not a full capacity for it. So we must first cultivate kindness toward people for whom this is easier, such as our own mother, relatives, or friends.

We begin by cultivating the loving-kindness we already have and then work on increasing it. Next, we should try to develop loving-kindness toward more difficult objects, like our enemies. We should attempt to transcend the superficial distinctions between people we see as friends, enemies, and those we treat with indifference. We should try to see that we have been closely related to all three—friends, enemies, and indifferent persons—at one time or another.

By understanding our relatedness to others, and seeing that everyone has given us much love and kindness as our relatives and friends, we can finally develop loving-kindness for all sentient beings indiscriminately. It is possible for us to wish all sentient beings to be happy and to have the cause of happiness. In this way we must cultivate and build up loving-kindness toward all.

After we develop loving-kindness we must next develop compassion. Compassion is generated by focusing on a particular sentient being that is suffering and wishing that this being be free from suffering and its causes. As in the meditation on loving-kindness, we start first with easier people and then gradually build up to more difficult ones, finally applying the meditation to all sentient beings.

On the basis of loving-kindness and compassion, then create enlightenment thought, also known as bodhicitta. Enlightenment thought is the resolution "For the sake of all sentient beings, I must attain perfect enlightenment and shall undertake the bodhisattva path." Loving-kindness and compassion are very essential. But loving-kindness and compassion without bodhicitta will not lead to ultimate enlightenment.

In order to be completely free from saṃsāra, one must completely cut the root of saṃsāra, which is self-clinging. In reality there is no self to cling to. Yet due to delusion, which we call dualism, we experience defilements, and through defilements we perform negative actions, which trap us in the realm of existence. We must create bodhicitta to crush self-clinging, which is the source of all suffering. In order to crush self-clinging, we must practice the two bodhicittas, which are known as *relative bodhicitta* and *absolute bodhicitta*. Relative bodhicitta can only suppress and deactivate self-clinging; absolute bodhicitta will completely eradicate self-clinging.

Relative bodhicitta has two parts: (1) wishing bodhicitta and (2) entering bodhicitta. *Wishing bodhicitta* means having a sincere wish to attain perfect enlightenment for the sake of all sentient beings. *Entering bodhicitta* means that you do not only wish to attain enlightenment; in order to achieve it, you are actually doing the practice and proceeding on the path. This implies entering the path and proceeding with practice. After developing the wish to achieve enlightenment, any effort you make in order to gain enlightenment, such as study, contemplation, and meditation, is considered entering bodhicitta.

At the beginning of this practice you should see others as equal to yourself. This is an important practice because we are in the habit of believing that there is an enormous difference between ourselves and others. No matter how much we care for others, we care far more for ourselves. Self-clinging is a propensity we have cultivated from beginningless time. Even when we consider another person "beloved," typically we still care more about ourselves, and self-clinging persists. To change this we must cultivate the practice of loving other beings as much as ourselves. Then gradually, as we habituate to this attitude, we become able to give up our own happiness, benefit, and other good things for the sake of other beings. Then we can begin to take others' sufferings and the cause of their sufferings onto ourselves. If we had done this in the past, we would already be enlightened. But from beginningless time until now, we have only cared for ourselves.

We care more for ourselves, so every effort we make is for our own sake—but this only manages to achieve more suffering. For this reason we begin to meditate on exchanging our happiness and others' suffering. First, we meditate on our dear ones and later we meditate on more difficult people, like our enemies, and finally we meditate on all sentient beings. In this way we accumulate merit and eradicate selfish thoughts as well as the habit of self-clinging.

Relative bodhicitta only suppresses self-clinging, so that the defilements become inactive. In this sense, the defilements are not eradicated but appear again in the future when the conditions are right. In order to completely eradicate the attitude of self-clinging, one needs to practice absolute bodhicitta. Absolute bodhicitta is the experience of absolute reality, the true nature of all phenomena. This is not the sort of thing ordinary people generally think about.

Intelligent people try to examine and draw conclusions about questions such as "What is the true nature of reality?" or "Why are we here?" This is the reason many different philosophical schools describing different views exist. Even in Buddhism we have different philosophical schools, such as Sarvāstivāda, Sautrāntika, Vibhajyavāda, and Madhyamaka. Within these there are also internal divisions.

The Madhyamaka (Middle Way) is the highest philosophical school. It was prophesied by the lord Buddha himself. The great Madhyamaka bhikṣu Nāgārjuna explained cause and effect and interdependent origination as relative truths. Nothing can independently exist due to the law of cause and effect; the result depends on its cause while the cause depends on its seed. Yet on the absolute level, as Nāgārjuna examined it with his very sharp logic, ultimate reality is beyond all extremes, such as existence, nonexistence, both, neither, and so on.

The ultimate truth is completely beyond our relative mind's perception or description. Yet these two truths do not contradict each other. The visions we see now are all interdependent. Things do not arise from no cause, the wrong cause, or an incomplete cause. Each and everything must have its own right and complete cause. And due to that cause, the result arises. In this way, we see things, hear them, taste them, and so forth. This is the relative vision. But on the absolute level, the same forms we see and sounds we hear are beyond all description and beyond all extremes. Nevertheless, these two truths do not contradict each other.

Concentration and Insight Meditation

The root of saṃsāra and nirvāṇa, happiness and suffering, is the mind. It is the mind that experiences suffering. It is the mind that experiences happiness. It is the mind that causes us to be born in this realm of existence. It is the mind that attains liberation and enlightenment. Since the root of all things is the mind, by realizing the true nature of mind, then the truth of all outer and inner phenomenon is realized. To give rise to this realization, you must practice concentration (*śamatha*) and insight wisdom (*vipaśyanā*).

By removing obscurations of thought and remaining in the true nature of mind, which is without obscuration and interference of thought, one enters a state of calmness that is known as concentration. Based on that, the practice of insight wisdom removes the curtain of duality. At present we see things in the duality of subject and object. Through the practice of insight wisdom meditation, the curtain of dualistic perception is removed and the true nature of mind is experienced.

According to the sūtras, concentration means that the mind remains in single-pointed focus without the interference of thoughts. Concentration is also known as calm abiding meditation, or *śamatha* in Sanskrit. Then, insight wisdom (or *vipaśyanā*) allows us to see the true state of reality. In order to achieve insight wisdom, first we must practice concentration.

Concentration

To practice concentration, we must be free from all outer and inner obstacles. Outer obstacles are attachments to activities and so on. Inner obstacles are defilements such as desire and hatred. You should practice concentration in a place where you are completely free from all activities. In order to practice correctly, it is important to know the five faults and to apply the eight antidotes and the nine methods.

The five faults are the following:

1. Laziness—you do not make the effort to practice virtuous deeds, especially meditation.
2. Forgetfulness—even if you try to practice, you forget the techniques or instructions you have been given.
3. Sinking and scattering—even if you do not forget the instructions on how to practice, your mind may be drowsy or heavy and not fully awake, which is called sinking. Alternatively, your mind may be so agitated that it cannot remain single-pointed due to thoughts and distraction, which is called scattering.
4. Incorrect application of the antidote—even though you know that your mind is veering into either sinking or scattering, you may not make the effort to apply the correct antidotes.
5. Overapplication of the antidote—due to the overapplication of antidotes, your meditation may become disturbed.

It is important to know these five faults so that you can apply the eight antidotes appropriately.

Laziness is the main fault in practicing concentration, and it has four main antidotes. The first is to have a strong intention to practice meditation. The second is to exert effort in bringing your mind to the point of actual concentration. The third is to have faith that if you practice this meditation, you will achieve results. The fourth is to think that by relying on the result of calm abiding through the practice of concentration, you will experience physical comfort and mental calmness. Of these four antidotes, the second (effort) is the most important. Actions that can be taken to remove laziness are remembering (1) the suffering of saṃsāra, (2) the difficulty of obtaining precious human birth, and (3) impermanence. Remembering these, you will remove laziness and bring your mind to actually do the meditation.

The antidote for the second fault, forgetfulness, is to mindfully remember the meditation techniques. When you receive the meditation instructions, carefully pay attention to them.

The third fault, mental sinking or scattering, is the main obstacle to meditation. You have to determine if your mind is sinking or scattering in order to apply the appropriate antidote.

The fourth fault is not applying the antidote. The antidote to this is to apply the appropriate antidote as soon as one's mind is scattering or sinking.

The fifth fault is overapplication of the antidote. For this we have to apply equanimity. It is important to maintain balance in every action and in every effort in order to fulfill our goal.

The root of all phenomena is the mind; if one realizes the true nature of mind, then one will realize all outer and inner phenomena. Therefore, it is important to understand and realize the true nature of the mind. Yet from beginningless time until now, our mind has developed strong propensities, defilements, and thoughts. Insight wisdom cannot be established when the mind is so busy. Therefore, concentration is very important.

The mind is brought to concentration using nine methods. It is difficult at first to concentrate on an internal object or visualization because the mind is constantly busy with different thoughts. So first place the mind on an outer object such as an image of a buddha or a flower or an object.

1. Place a solid object on a table about two feet away from the eyes. Concentrate on that object through the eyes, mind, and breath. Do not blink the eyes or move the body. When meditating, do not think about the quality of the object or its shape or color. Just place and hold the mind on the unmoving object without the interference of other thoughts.
2. Continually focus the mind. It is difficult for beginners to concentrate for a long period of time, so it is advisable to keep each session short and repeat the session several times.
3. Watch for and recognize distraction. Sometimes during meditation, the mind may become distracted, yet we do not even notice it. It is important to recognize distractions and instantly bring the mind back to the concentration object and continue the meditation.

4. Be mindful. Remain mindful throughout the session so that the mind does not scatter or sink.
5. Tame the mind. Remember the great qualities and benefits of meditation in order to motivate yourself to do this meditation.
6. Pacify the mind. If an outer distraction occurs during meditation, keep placing the mind on the concentration object. Even if the distraction persists, pacify the mind and continue to place it on the meditation object.
7. Eliminate thoughts. If thoughts like desire or hatred arise during meditation, place the mind back on the meditation object and eliminate those negative thoughts.
8. Remain single-pointed. If the mind remains agitated despite applying the antidotes, continue to eliminate the emotions and bring the concentration back to the meditation object.
9. Be persistent. When we first practice this meditation, lots of difficulties arise. But by continuing this practice every day, it will become easier. Eventually you will be able to place the mind on an object and remain in meditation without much effort. You will experience many concrete benefits, such as tranquility, calmness, peace of mind, and great physical and mental comfort.

We have explained how to do concentration, or śamatha meditation, by knowing the five faults, applying the eight antidotes to those faults, and also applying the nine methods. The first experience that arises when practicing concentration meditation is the surfacing of many thoughts, one after another. Do not be discouraged at this stage. Normally, we do not notice how many thoughts are constantly arising within our mind. Meditation allows us to realize how busy our mind is. Therefore, this stage is actually the first level of experience when your meditation is effective. It is known as the "experience of recognizing thoughts." It spurs us to continue meditation practice.

As we continue to practice, thoughts still arise but there are some gaps in between. This is the second stage of experience, which is called the "experience of thoughts resting." In the third stage, although thoughts do arise, there will be calmness and clarity between the thoughts, and while experiencing that calmness and clarity, again thoughts will arise. In the fourth stage there is more calmness and clarity in the mind, and the intervals without any thoughts grow longer and longer, like a consistently calm ocean with only an occasional wave arising. Still we continue with the practice. Finally, in the fifth stage, all thoughts in the mind cease and the mind resides single-pointedly, experiencing calm and peace, like an ocean without waves.

But resting in calm abiding is not the same as experiencing clarity. The next aim is to remain in the tranquility of single-pointed concentration while at the same time experiencing clarity, like the light of a candle unstirred by wind, completely steady and clear. When this experience is achieved, the practice is repeated without an outer object, concentrating on the clarity of awareness itself. If obstacles like scattering and sinking still arise, then continue the practice through the application of method.

If we do concentration practice in this way, gradually single-pointed concentration will be attained.

Insight Meditation

After one has attained the ability to dwell in total calmness and clarity, then begin to practice insight meditation. Without insight meditation, the practice of methods such as loving-kindness, compassion, and morality only suppresses but does not eradicate the faults.

In order to completely eradicate the source of the faults, which is self-clinging, and to completely awake from illusion, it is necessary to cultivate wisdom. Through the combination of method (also known as skillful means) and wisdom, enlightenment can be attained. In order to fly in the sky, we need two wings. In order to cross the road, we need both eyes to see and feet to walk. Similarly, in order to attain enlightenment, we need both method and wisdom.

The main fault that traps us in the realm of existence is self-clinging. At the moment, without authentic logical reasons, we cling to our present form and consciousness as our "self." But if we carefully and logically examine this belief, we cannot find a self anywhere.

If there were self, it would have to be the name, the body, or the mind. Of course, our name is not our self because it could be given to anybody.

The body is also not the self because "the body" refers to the aggregation of many different parts, such as skin, bones, muscles, organs, and so on. The mind is also not the self because it is changing moment by moment; to call the mind the self is like thinking that a colorful rope is a snake. Until we realize the colorful rope is not a snake, we feel anxiety and fear. Likewise, until we realize the self has no true existence, we unavoidably cling to this realm of existence. In order to be completely free from all these illusions, we need to cut the root of saṃsāra, which is self-clinging. To do this, we need wisdom that is completely beyond ordinary thought and wisdom that realizes selflessness.

All outer and inner things have no self. All outer objects are not real. Many teachings explain that all the phenomena we experience are an illusion. Moreover, logically, if all outer objects existed independently, then they should appear the same to everyone. Yet this is not the case. For example, for some people a certain place is a happy place, whereas for others, the same place is unhappy. Different people have different experiences depending on the level of their minds. This observation is too profound and deep for us to meditate on straightaway, but we can build this understanding gradually.

Ultimate reality is away from all extremes and descriptions because, as Nāgārjuna explained, everything is interdependent. Because of interdependence, everything is emptiness. Because of emptiness, everything is interdependent.

Every activity in saṃsāra and nirvāṇa is possible because everything is emptiness. This view is known in the Lamdré teaching as "the non-differentiation of saṃsāra and nirvāṇa." This means that any object the conventional mind perceives, if it is seen analytically free from delusion, can be perceived as ultimate reality. Our ordinary minds perceive sounds, flavors, and sights merely as sounds we hear, food we taste, and things we see. However, great bodhisattvas, beings who have already achieved realization and are free from delusion, will perceive those same objects as ultimate reality.

For example, we see a cup simply as a cup, but after going through careful logical examination, contemplation, meditation, and realization, a great bodhisattva will see the same cup as ultimate reality. Great bodhisattvas who have already attained realization see ultimate reality, whereas we of ordinary defiled mind see it as a cup or ordinary object. In actuality there are not two separate realities; it is the same cup.

We of ordinary mind have impure vision, but the great beings view the same object as ultimate reality or nirvāṇa. We of ordinary mind view the world we are experiencing as saṃsāra, while with wisdom, which is free from illusion, the same world is viewed as ultimate reality, nirvāṇa. That is the reason that there is no difference between saṃsāra and nirvāṇa at the ultimate level. In this way one can say that what the ordinary mind sees is conventional, or relative, truth. Relative truth is all things as we see and feel them now. And this same relative truth we see now will become ultimate truth when we have attained realization through meditation.

This ultimate reality is the vision of clarity. It is different from emptiness as viewed by the ordinary, relative mind. Appearances are something we see, while emptiness means there is nothing to see. These two appear contradictory, but in reality they do not contradict. Clarity is not separate from emptiness and emptiness is not separate from clarity. Ultimate reality is within every sentient being, but we do not recognize it. Those who do not recognize it cling to the idea of a self and get caught up in the illusory vision, which is known as saṃsāra. Those who realize this ordinary world as an illusion and are awakened from it experience the pure vision, which is known as nirvāṇa. The difference between saṃsāra and nirvāṇa lies in whether we have achieved realization or not; from the point of view of the object itself, there is neither saṃsāra to abandon nor nirvāṇa to achieve.

To realize this is to realize the nondifferentiation of saṃsāra and nirvāṇa. But we ordinary people cannot practice this immediately, as we have a very strong propensity to cling to this world as real. For example, even on a mundane level, even though we know our bad habits will eventually yield serious consequences, they are difficult to give up. Since we have this subtle yet very strong propensity to cling to the world, it is very difficult for us to meditate straight away on emptiness, ultimate reality, or absolute bodhicitta. Instead, we have to do it gradually.

The first step in training the mind to perceive ultimate reality is to establish all appearances as our own mind. There are eight examples to illustrate this point.

The first example of how all appearances are our own mind is dreams. Let us compare recent dreams, which we can clearly remember, to the ordinary life we go through. We find that there is no difference between the two. In dreams, we experience happiness and suffering, and we talk and remember what we did very clearly. But when we awaken, there is no sign of what we saw in the dream. Similarly, in this ordinary life, when all the strong propensities habituated in the consciousness ripen, combined with causes and conditions, we see things. But in reality, there is no difference between dreams and our present life.

The second example is the effect of substances. After taking certain hallucinogenic substances, we experience completely different visions than the life we normally live. Due to the effect of the substances, we have feelings and experiences as strong as in ordinary life. In reality, the life we are going through is the same as a dream or being under the influence of hallucinogenic substances. But due to our strong propensities, our ordinary mind sees a vast difference between the experiences.

The third example is illness. When we have a high fever we may see different things.

The fourth example is the effect of spirits. The person under the influence of certain spirits will behave, experience, and say different things as though what he is experiencing is real.

The fifth example is the effect of pressing the corner of your eyes. For some people, even without doing this, if they look in a certain way or have certain vision problems, such as double vision, they also see things differently.

The sixth example is cataracts, in which people see hairs before their eyes, resulting in having a different vision of the world. If that vision were real, then everyone would see it, but since only certain people see it, then it is not real.

The seventh example is the fiery ring that appears when we twirl a torch in a circle. In reality, there is really no continuous ring, but due to the visual residue, a ring appears to our eyes. If we logically analyze the ring, when the torch is in one place, it is not in the other places in the ring. But it appears everywhere at once. This shows that seeing something is not logical proof that it exists. Even in the relative level we see things that do not exist.

The eighth example is that if you turn around in circles very fast and then stop, the world also seems to turn.

Remember these examples, reflect on them, and then meditate to establish that all appearances are visions of our own mind. Even on the mundane level, it is quite clear that the mind is the most important factor in what we see.

The second step is to establish all mental appearances as a magical show. This view has many different supporting examples. One example is how, by using certain substances, movements, or methods, a magician or hypnotist can make things like animals and houses appear. Although we understand these to be illusory magical shows, we experience them as reality, as real as our present life. In fact, on the ultimate level, all our mental visions are like an unreal magical show and are not real. When all the causes and conditions come together, a magical show appears. If any of the causes or conditions is missing, then it will not appear.

All appearances are a magical show that is devoid of self-nature. All inner mental experience and all outer objects—everything is like a magical show, which is the nonduality of appearance and emptiness. Appearance and emptiness, although very different on the relative level, ultimately do not contradict one another. Appearance is emptiness, and emptiness is appearance. The two are not separate.

The third step is to establish that all phenomena are devoid of self-nature. This process has two parts.

The first step in establishing all phenomena as devoid of self-nature is to establish all phenomena as interdependently originated. A result depends on its cause and a cause depends on its result. This has many examples. For instance, if you plant a tree on fertile ground with the right moisture, right temperature, and good seed, then it starts growing. But if the seed is in a dry place without the necessary temperature and soil, then it will not grow. This is a very good example of interdependent origination, because a fruit appears neither without its seed, nor from the wrong seed, nor from an incomplete seed. In order for a result to arise, you need each and every cause and condition. You need both the right causes and the complete causes.

In the same way, in the past we committed many virtuous and nonvirtuous actions. These caused habituated propensities, which are like seeds planted in the fertile ground of our mind. The ripening of these seeds gave rise to the life we are going through. Until all the right causes and conditions meet together, these experiences will not arise. In other words, at this time we have the karma, the causes, and the propensities to see the world as a human being. But when we die, this vision will cease and another completely different vision will appear. In reality, none of these experiences that we go through truly exist. But at the same time, this vision continues until we realize the reality of emptiness. All things are interdependent. Because of interdependence, all things are emptiness.

The next step after establishing all phenomena as devoid of self-nature is to establish all interdependently originated phenomena as inexpressible. As I explained in the beginning, ultimate reality is away from all descriptions and extremes. After careful logical examination, various philosophical schools have come to different conclusions or views. One of these is the view that objects do not exist, only the mind exists—which is the Mind-Only school's position. But the highest Madhyamaka (or Middle Way) view is that the ultimate is beyond all description as either existent, nonexistent, both, or neither.

We experience all outer objects as mental appearances and all mental appearances as magical shows that are interdependent. You cannot describe your experiences, just as babies cannot explain why they smile. Similarly, ultimate reality can be experienced but not described.

Ordinary people see things in duality, separating the subject and object, but this is not ultimate reality. Ultimate reality is beyond this curtain of duality. After tearing away the curtain of dualistic vision, all phenomena are seen as ultimate reality, which is itself away from any description. This ultimate reality, or absolute truth, is everywhere and is the true nature of all phenomena.

Ultimate reality is also the true nature of the mind. This is also called buddha nature, and everyone possesses it. But until we meet the right conditions we cannot realize this, and instead, we cling to a self and continue to suffer in this realm of existence.

Many higher tantric teachings call ultimate reality "simultaneously born primordial wisdom." The word *simultaneous* is used here to mean that the result and the cause arise simultaneously and the result is not elsewhere than the cause. In this sense, the result is not something we seek outside ourselves but is actually within ourselves. Because the cause and the result are simultaneously born, buddha nature is within every human being. If we make efforts, we can all attain full enlightenment.

In the relative sense, we go through different phases along the path to enlightenment. However, we must understand that there is a continuity between our ordinary cause mind and the ultimate enlightenment mind. We might consider the example of a copper container that is used to hold excrement. Used in such a way, we consider the copper dirty. But if the same copper were melted down and made into ornaments that people wear proudly and others admire, we would consider the copper beautiful. If again the ornaments were melted down and made into the image of a deity, then the same copper would become a precious object of worship and respect. The point is that the actual nature of the copper never changes. The same copper has been used as a container for filth, as an ornament, and as the statue of a deity. Similarly, the true nature of our mind is buddha nature. The true state of all phenomena is that same ultimate reality. Through practice and the application of method and wisdom, obscurations can be eliminated and realization achieved.

The common vision of experience is the result of the practice of common yogas, whereas the uncommon vision of experience arises through uncommon yoga meditation, particularly tantric practices, which require proper transmission and blessings. We ordinary sentient beings, after practice, can each become a yogi endowed with the vision of experience.

The Pure Vision

After the vision of experience, when all obscurations have been gradually eliminated and inner wisdom fully dawns, then the third vision—the pure vision—is experienced: this is the ultimate attainment of enlightenment.

The buddhas have abandoned every possible fault or obscuration and through great realizations achieved the pure vision. Just as a man who has awakened from sleep no longer experiences his dreams, similarly, beings who are completely awakened from illusion no longer see the impure vision. It is the same world we reside in now, but—perceived through completely pure vision—it becomes pure primordial wisdom.

8. Biographies of Great Sakya Women and Their Early Contemporaries

Biographies of Great Disciples of Drokmi Lotsāwa

Drokmi Lotsāwa (992–1072 c.e.) brought the Lamdré teaching from India to Tibet. He had seven disciples who reached the great attainment of the stage of siddhas. Three were men and four were women. Their holy biographies are here translated by Venerable Khenpo Kalsang Gyaltsen and Chodrungma Kunga Chodron from the Lamdré Kokphup Lekshé Düpai Gyatso *by Sakyapa Ngawang Künga Sönam.*

Gyergom Sewo

The first of Drokmi Lotsāwa's disciples was Gyergom Sewo, from Tsang. He was the son of a wealthy family and very intelligent. When he heard the good qualities of Lachen Drokmi Lotsāwa, he was very moved, and so traveled to meet him, taking along many material offerings, including a fine sword, and requested instruction. Drokmi Lotsāwa observed that conditions were very auspicious and told Gyergom Sewo, "You may be able to win the battle with saṃsāra." He agreed to give him instruction, and began by giving him three major empowerments, one after the other, and then continued to teach him for three years, including the bestowal of a prophecy at the end of the teachings.

In appreciation for having received the teaching, Gyergom Sewo offered a hundred bags of grain. Then, for thirteen years, he did retreat in Taklo Ding and other places. Through this, he achieved very high realization, unobstructed clairvoyance, and the ability to perform miracles. Finally, saying, "I have no connection with disciples in Tibet," he departed to the glorious mountain of Śrīparvata.

Shengom Rokpo

Shengom Rokpo was from Tsang Tanak, and his uncle was a strong practitioner of the Bön religion. After his uncle died, Shengom Rokpo went to where his uncle used to live, and the uncle's disciples offered him many material things. Most of the things he used for the funeral and rituals for his uncle. The remaining things he exchanged for thirteen gold coins.

Shengom Rokpo had heard of the many good qualities of Drokmi Lotsāwa but had some distrust of the Bön religion. Taking along the gold, he and seven companions went to meet Drokmi Lotsāwa. He offered all the gold to Drokmi Lotsāwa and requested the Lamdré teaching. For five years, Drokmi Lotsāwa bestowed upon him the Lamdré teaching, and at the end of the teaching, he bestowed upon him a prophecy of attainment.

Then Shengom Rokpo went to northern Semodo, where he meditated for thirteen years. There he achieved the stage of a mahāsiddha. After reaching that stage, through his clairvoyance, he saw that in the area of Mount Kailash there were many Bön practitioners and that if he were to give them instruction, he would be able to send them to the Khecari realm. Saying thus, he departed at sunset for Mount Kailash, using the sun's rays as a vehicle.

Üpa Dröpoché

Üpa Dröpoché was from Phenyül Rakma. Earlier in his life, he was the powerful and fierce bandit Tresé, the leader of a group of a hundred bandits that he had gathered around him. They stole things from the nomads in the north and sold them in Lhasa, and then stole things from Lhasa and sold them in the north. Once he also indulged himself with his sister, and his sister became with child. Shamed by this, he stole turquoise and other things from his family and ran away to Tsang.

Reaching Tsang, he heard of the good qualities of Drokmi Lotsāwa, and a karmic connection was awakened within him. He traveled to Mugulung

Valley where he met the great lama Drokmi. He offered all of the turquoise and other things to him and requested Dharma teachings. Drokmi realized that he had the prerequisites necessary to be a suitable vessel for the teachings. After bestowing initiation and instructions, he prepared Üpa Dröpoché to do meditation.

Through meditation Üpa Dröpoché attained very fine experience and realization. His internal air became as powerful as a sharpened razor, and due to this strength, he could digest anything he ate. At every meal, he consumed three *dré* (roughly one and a half gallons) of *tsampa*. He continued to meditate and finally achieved the stage of a mahāsiddha, then departed for the mountain Śrīparvata.

Dregoma Konné

Dregoma Konné was the daughter of a family from Dré Kharbu. She was sent as a bride to her husband's family, and after one year of marriage, her husband passed away. She mourned very deeply. In her mental agony, she experienced the gathering of her elements, and sobbed loudly for very long periods of time.

Once, while she was sobbing thus, Lachen Drokmi was on his way home from a gathering and heard her. He inquired who she was and someone explained her story. Remarking that she had probably produced the experience of self-arising mourning, Lachen Drokmi said that if her relatives brought her to see him at his home, he would give her some instruction. The next day, four people carried Dregoma Konné to where Lachen Drokmi lived in Mugulung. He gave her instructions on dispelling hindrances, and her hindrances were removed.

After that, Drokmi Lotsāwa asked, "Dregoma, has your meditative experience increased?"

She answered, "Did you give me instructions on how to meditate? I have completely forgotten everything, even how many days I have been here."

The lama said, "This is a good sign. Not remembering anything is also known as the mental state free of conception that recalls the good qualities of the Buddha, Dharma, and Saṅgha."

Then Drokmi Lotsāwa gave her the oral instructions of the water crystal jewel. After meditating on that for a while, Dregoma Konné remained in a single session of meditation for twenty-four hours. When she arose from the session, Drokmi Lotsāwa gave her empowerment, explanation, and instructions on meditation beyond thought. Within that teaching is a verse that says:

> Under the influence of the eye consciousness,
> Arises the great wonder of nondual primordial wisdom.
> Through practicing both of these,
> The wisdom of nonduality blazes.

Based on these words, strong meditation arose within her. At Drokmi Lotsāwa's Dharma gathering at Mugulung, Dregoma Konné remained in a single session of meditation for seven days without moving. She became an exemplar of a disciple who was able to gather the elements through the blessings of the path of devotion. She continued to meditate and attained the stage of a mahāsiddha without abandoning her body. For some time, she meditated on Jomo Nakgyal Mountain, in the Podong Range. There, *yakṣas* sponsored her food and service. Later, she departed to Oḍḍiyāna.

Tömo Dorjetso

Tömo Dorjetso was born in Mangkhar Tötso. She was sent as a bride to a man named Dro Dradul and bore seven sons. One day, bandits attacked the family, killed all seven of her sons and her husband, and stole all of their possessions. In her grief, she lost consciousness and after five days had still not awakened.

Her relatives asked Lachen Drokmi Lotsāwa for advice, and he told them, "I am an expert at restoring those who have lost consciousness, so bring her here." She was carried to the lama, and when Drokmi Lotsāwa gave her blessings, she awoke.

Immediately Drokmi Lotsāwa taught her how to meditate, which she did according to his instructions, producing good experience and realization. She continued to meditate on that experience and achieved very high realization and attainment. She departed to the Khecari realm without leaving her body and became an exemplar of a disciple who manifested the natural gathering of elements in those with karmic connections.

Shapamo Chamchik

Shapamo Chamchik was from Tsamorong. She was the daughter of Lord Gyalpo and was the only sister among seven brothers. She had very strong faith in the Dharma and was very intelligent. Once she visited Lachen Drokmi, bringing many material offerings, and requested instruction. Lama Drokmi Lotsāwa was very pleased and immediately gave her empowerment.

During the third empowerment, the lama introduced her to the simultaneous arising of liquid bliss. She immediately recognized it and remained in that meditative experience until midmorning of the next day. When she arose, she prostrated before Drokmi Lotsāwa and offered this expression of her appreciation: "I met the guru, the real Buddha, and immediately received blessings. I found the Buddha from the mind itself. Without abandoning the realm of saṃsāra, I have purified it. I have already accomplished the great goal."

She continued to meditate on that experience, and by the age of twenty-five, she attained the ability to perform miracles and clairvoyance, afterward departing for Oḍḍiyāna.

Chemo Namkha

Chemo Namkha was the older sister of Drom Depa Tönchung. The Drom family had five brothers—Lama Trogyal Yeshé, depa Śākya Gyal, depa Tönchung, Özer Dorjé, and another brother. Chemo Namkha was the oldest sibling. One day, all the brothers had the same dream: Many women appeared and asked them, "Won't you please send your sister Namkha Yeshé to Drokmi Lotsāwa's place with many material offerings? From there, she will reach Khecari and we will lead her to that place."

Around that time, Chemo Namkha lost consciousness for three days. When she awoke, she recounted many holy deeds of Drokmi Lotsāwa. Her parents and other relatives were amazed. They gathered together many material offerings and sent her to Lachen Drokmi Lotsāwa.

At that time, Drokmi Lotsāwa was staying in Mangsang Cave in Namthang Karpo. While he was teaching the Dharma to his disciples, a young woman with many auspicious signs arrived and said to him, "I begged permission of my parents to be allowed to come to visit you." Saying this, she offered an extremely valuable turquoise as well as many other material offerings. She begged him, "Please send me to Khecari."

That very evening, Lachen Drokmi gave her and her friends the empowerment of Cakrasaṃvara, followed by instructions on closing the upper aperture. Immediately, Chemo Namkha was able to cause her air and mind to enter the central channel, and the signs that they had entered the channel became evident.

Chemo Namkha told her friends, "I have already had some indication that I will be able to immediately reach the Khecari realm. Please go back home and explain to my parents that I have had this experience."

Drokmi Lotsāwa gave her Dharma teachings on Vajravārāhī, the creation stage of Vajrayoginī, and the completion stage of Avadhūti. As a supplement to this path, to promote the common attainments, he also taught her the practices of the female yakṣinī Padmapati, the controlling Kölpo Padaka, and the method of extracting the nutrition of great medicine.

Through practice of these instructions, she was able to control the yakṣas, and for a long time stayed in central Tibet in the area known as Shundrakrum Passage. There she built a little retreat cabin. When people came to the cabin, she would pull balls of tsampa dough and draughts of *chang* beer from space, and would distribute them to as many people as came. Later, she departed for the Khecari realm.

Disciples of Sachen Künga Nyingpo for Whom His Eleven Commentaries on the Precious Lamdré Teaching Were Composed

Among the innumerable disciples of Sachen Künga Nyingpo, there were eleven for whom he composed a complete Lamdré teaching. These eleven commentaries and the disciples for whom they were composed are described in the Lamdré Kokphup Lekshé Düpai Gyatso *by Sakyapa Ngawang Künga Sönam and are translated here by Venerable Khenpo Kalsang Gyaltsen and Chodrung-ma Kunga Chodron.*

Sachen Künga Nyingpo's first commentary was composed for the disciple Aseng, who was the first to request the Lamdré teaching from him. The title of the Lamdré commentary composed for Aseng was *Asengma.*

The second commentary was composed for the disciple Shujé Ngödrup. The title of the Lamdré commentary composed for him is *Shujema.*

The third commentary was composed for the son of the noble family Chödrak from Lokya. Therefore, the title of this Lamdré commentary is known as *Lokyama.*

The fourth commentary was composed for Sachen Künga Nyingpo's first consort, Machik Tsetsa, the mother of his oldest son, Künga Bar. She was a daughter of the Tibetan royal lineage. After her son Künga Bar passed away, Machik Tsetsa became interested in spiritual things, and she received the Hevajra and Cakrasaṃvara empowerments from Sachen Künga Nyingpo. Especially for her, he used Cakrasaṃvara as a creation practice, with the completion practice according to the Lamdré Hevajra. The commentary on the Lamdré teaching that was composed for her is known as *Yumdönma* (For the Mother).

Sachen Künga Nyingpo wrote the fifth commentary for his sons Sönam Tsemo and Jetsün Drakpa, and for his heart disciple Nyen Phuljungwa Tsuktor Gyalpo (whose common name was Sönam Dorjé). Because it was written for these three sons, it is known as *Sedönma* (For the Sons).

The sixth commentary was composed for the Bodhisattva Dawa Gyaltsen, who received the bodhisattva vow from Künga Nyingpo. Dawa Gyaltsen transmitted the *upāsikā* vow to Künga Nyingpo's two sons. Künga Nyingpo composed for him the Lamdré commentary known as *Dagyalma.*

The seventh commentary was composed for his disciple Sangri Phukpa, and it is therefore known as *Sangriphukma.*

The eighth commentary was composed for the nun from Mangkhar known as Mangchungma, and so it is also known as *Mangchungma.* Another source, *History of the Precious Lamdré Teaching,* provides more information about Mangchungma.

Mangchungma was one of the seven chief disciples of Sachen Künga Nyingpo who were considered to have achieved the stage of patience. Those seven disciples were as follows: Jetsün Drakpa Gyaltsen, Shujé Ngödrup, Yogi Sönam Gyaltsen from Nyak, the Yogi from Tsarkha, Dorjé Drak from Ga, Yogi Ödrak, and Yoginī Mangchungma.

Mangchungma was born in Kara. After receiving teachings, she meditated at Samling according to Sachen Künga Nyingpo's instructions. While meditating, she achieved the experience of the purification of animal realms. Especially, perceptions of yaks arose. Whatever she saw on a road or in the valley, she perceived in the form of a yak, and she perceived many of them stampeding toward her. She tried to escape but could not, and she was trampled by them. This caused her to awaken from that experience, and because the experience was excessively vivid, she could literally see yaks moving about.

After this, all of her perceptions arose as bliss. Soft things such as clothing or cushions, hard things such as stones, and sharp things such as thorns all arose as great bliss. As a result of this, she no longer experienced discomfort or displeasure. She remained meditating in this state for the rest of her life, and achieved very high realization.

Sachen Künga Nyingpo's two sons were his principal disciples. However, his son Lopön Rinpoché Sönam Tsemo is not counted as his disciple, because he was of equal realization. Other than Sönam Tsemo, the seven disciples who achieved the stage of patience were considered of equal realization.

The ninth commentary was composed for a disciple from Kham who limped, so it is known as *Gathengma* (For the Limper from Ga).

The tenth commentary was composed for a nun from Yarlung, who was known as Auma, and the commentary bears her name, *Auma*.

The eleventh commentary was composed for Wangchuk Gyaltsen from Nyakshi and is known as *Nyakma*.

In this way, Sachen Künga Nyingpo composed eight Lamdré commentaries for men disciples and three for women. These are his eleven commentaries on the Precious Lamdré teaching.

The great lama Sachen Künga Nyingpo had innumerable disciples. Among them, the greatest was Lopön Sönam Tsemo, who was Sachen

Künga Nyingpo's physical as well as spiritual son. Even as a child, Lopön Sönam Tsemo reached the stage of a first bodhisattva bhūmi. When he departed this life, he simultaneously manifested two different methods of passing into *parinirvāṇa*.

As prophesied by Lama Shangtön and in accordance with Sachen Künga Nyingpo's own dream at the time of receiving the preliminary Hevajra initiation from Khön Gyichuwa, Sachen Künga Nyingpo had three disciples who achieved the excellent attainment of mahāmudrā in this life and seven who achieved the stage of patience.

The three disciples who achieved the excellent attainment of mahāmudrā within this life were a yogi from Sri Lanka, the bodhisattva Tak, and Gompa Kyibar. The seven who achieved the stage of patience were Jetsün Rinpoché Drakpa Gyaltsen, Shujé, Dorjé Drak from Ga, Sönam Gyaltsen from Nyak, a meditator from Tsarkha, Gompa Ödrak, and the yoginī Mangchungma. There were countless other highly learned disciples, meditators who possessed great power, and excellent practitioners who remained in everyday life as hidden yogis. The biographies of most of these students are recounted in the *History of the Precious Lamdré Teaching*.

Sachen Künga Nyingpo had eleven heart disciples who received and upheld the lineage of oral instructions of the Lamdré, and seven heart disciples who wrote commentaries on his writings. There were four well-known great masters who accomplished both learning and realization. They are referred to in the homage written by Shujé. He wrote, "Eight men and three women received the instructions in writing."

The eight men were Aseng from Kham; Shujé from Lhopa; Chödrak, who was the son of a noble family; Sachen Künga Nyingpo's heart disciple Nyen Phuljungwa Tsuktor Gyalpo, who was also known as Sönam Dorjé; the Bodhisattva Dawa Gyaltsen, who was an emanation of Avalokiteśvara; Sangri Phukpa; Gatheng from Kham; and Wangchuk Gyaltsen from Nyakshi.

The three women were Chocham Purmo, who was his own consort and the mother of Künga Bar; Auma, who was a yoginī from Yarlung; and Mangchungma who was from Mangkhar. Among his disciples who received the Lamdré teaching, they are the best, and the ones for whom he wrote a special Lamdré teaching.

A Short Account of the Life of Jetsün Chimé Tenpai Nyima

This is a short account taken from an answer given by His Holiness Kyabgon Gongma Trichen Rinpoche in response to a question asked by his elder sister, her Eminence Jetsun Chimey Luding. It is condensed from the accounts of the lineage gurus.

Jetsün Chimé Tenpai Nyima lived some three hundred years ago and is one of the Vajrayoginī lineage gurus. She was an outstanding master, the guru of many masters—mostly Sakya, but from other schools as well. She was the teacher of many lineage holders and sons of the Khön family and many great khenpos.

Jetsünma Chimé Tenpai Nyima is among the lineage masters of *Parting from the Four Attachments* and of many other profound dharmas such as Vajrayoginī.

Her father, Thutob Wangchuk, was the younger brother of Sachen Künga Lodrö. Her mother was Tashi Yangchen, the daughter of a Chak Zampa landholder family. She was born in the Fire Mouse year of the thirteenth Rabjung cycle, which is 1756, and it was on the twenty-second day of the eleventh Tibetan month.

The name of her youth was Chimé Butri. In the year of the Water Tiger (1782), the twenty-fifth khenpo of the Great Temple, Jampa Chökyi Tashi, gave her ordination as a nun and bestowed the name Chimé Tenpai Nyima.

From the time of her youth, her father's brother Sachen Künga Lodrö directly taught her the oral transmissions of the collection of the *Lamdré Tsokshé* and *Lamdré Lopshé*, as well as the entirety of the collection of the profound teachings of Vajrayoginī. In this way, absorbing the teachings in the manner of water being poured from one vase to the next, she became owner of the practices of the ocean of vast and profound Dharma.

Sachen Künga Lodrö, in his pure vision, received a prophecy from Ngorchen Dorjé Chang saying, "You will have disciples like four pillars and eight beams." Chimé Nyima was one of these four great pillars who were the principal disciples. With heartfelt effort, she devoted all her life to daily practice, so that she reached a high level of realization. She also turned the vast and profound wheel of Dharma of the precious great secret *Lamdré Lopshé*, the Vajrayoginī cycle of teachings, the twelve maṇḍalas of *Sarvadurgatipariśodhana Tantra*, and many others. She performed innumerable great empowerments, authorizations, and so on, both of the tantra collections and of the profound and extensive teaching cycles. She directly bestowed teachings and empowerments to Dolma Phodrang's founding father and throneholder Pema Düdul Wangchuk and his heir, the throneholder Tashi Rinchen. Other disciples of hers include Phuntsok Phodrang's founding father Künga Rinchen and his son, and the throneholder Dorjé Rinchen; the brothers of these two founding fathers, Kyabgön Ngödrub Palbar and Ngawang Künga Gyaltsen; Thartsé Khenchen; Jampa Namkha Chimé; Jampa Künga Gyaltsen; Jampa Künga Tenzin; and Ācārya Künga Tashi of the Balkhang family. There were many others. At that time, all of the masters who held the Sakya and Ngorpa teachings were her disciples.

Her main disciple was the meditation master Ngawang Rinchen of Dergé. To him she gave the profound Vajrayoginī teaching at a time when she was already very old and had poor eyesight. But then, due to the pure mutual perception between master and disciple, her eyes became clear. On this occasion she said, "Seeing lamas like you in Tibet has restored my eyesight."

At one time during the Vajrayoginī blessing the nectar in the *kapala* bubbled vigorously and actually started to boil. The meditation master Ngawang Rinchen drank it again and again, and from this a high meditative experience was aroused in his mindstream. Many such amazing stories about her spread in all directions. Many practitioners particularly from Kham sought the blessings of her Vajrayoginī lineage, even if they were unable to actually meet with her.

Many high lamas such as Jamyang Khyentsé Wangpo asserted that Jetsün Chimé Nyima was the real Vajrayoginī in person. They said this and many other words of great praise. It is recorded in the accounts that at the time of Sachen Künga Lodrö's death Jetsünma herself did Vajrayoginī ritual sessions for many days.

Although the time of her death is not given clearly in the texts, we can judge that she must have lived a very long time because, starting from

Sachen Künga Lodrö's time, there are four generations of lamas to whom she gave empowerments. In later life, she stayed in Rikzin Phodrang and was called "Great Mother of Rikzin Phodrang."

After her death a silver Vajrayoginī image with many matchless uncommon ornaments was made in her honor. This is at the great temple in Sakya.

His Holiness Kyabgon Gongma Trichen Rinpoche Remembers Great Sakya Jetsünmas

There have been very great female Sakya practitioners ever since the earliest days of the lineage. Many were Jetsünmas—daughters of the Khön family. Here I recount some of the stories of those that I knew or heard about.

Jetsün Tadrin Wangmo

Jetsün Kalsang Chökyi Nyima was also known as Jetsünma Tadrin Wangmo. She was one of the famous Jetsünmas from the Phuntsok Phodrang branch of the Sakyapa tradition. There is a great deal of information regarding Tadrin Wangmo in the Sakya lineage history—a full chapter.

In addition to being a great practitioner, she was also a guru and from all accounts quite beautiful. It so happens that she was my grandfather's main guru, one of the most important gurus from whom he received *Lamdré Lopshé* and the Vajrayoginī cycle of teachings, along with the Vajramālā cycle of empowerments. My grandfather always used to refer to her as Vajrayoginī in person. Exact dates of her birth and passing away are not known.

She traveled within the Kham region for some time. Because Kham is so far away from Sakya, it was very difficult and very rare for people there to go to Sakya and receive the blessings of the Khön lineage. So when she traveled to Sakya, people felt very great devotion, especially the Sakyapas in Kham.

One story involves her travels to Trihor, east of Dergé. Nowadays, Trihor is in Sichuan. The local governor there was not a good man, being a womanizer who was always chasing beautiful women. And when he heard that Tadrin Wangmo was attracting so many followers, he decided that he wanted to meet her. She had a reputation as being a very holy teacher but, as I mentioned earlier, also very beautiful. So Tadrin Wangmo received a message that the governor wanted to meet her and that she should set a time for him to come. Her attendant was alarmed and told Tadrin Wangmo that they should leave, as he was a bad man and might harm her. But Jetsünma said, "No, it doesn't matter. You can make an appointment. He can come to see me. It's all right, there won't be any problem." So the appointment was made.

On that day, he appeared and entered Jetsünma's room to offer her a *khata*, in a very nervous manner. After that he rushed out of the room, shaking like a leaf. His attendant asked him, "Why did you leave so quickly? Yesterday you were so eager to meet Jetsünma, and now you just left straight away. Why did you do this?" The governor said, "Oh, she looked terrifying! She had a human body, but with the face of a pig, one with long tusks!" Thus she showed she was a real Vajravārāhī.

Another time, while she was traveling in the Kham area, her party came to a place where there were many bandits, some of which stole all the horses and mules that carried their luggage. Everyone in the party wanted to go and get the animals back. But she said, "No, this won't be necessary." She did a Mahākāla ritual, whereupon suddenly black dogs and black birds appeared from everywhere and surrounded the bandits' tents, threatening them and frightening them. They were so terrified that they immediately brought all the stolen horses and mules back to Jetsünma!

Jetsun Pema Trinley

Jetsunma Pema Trinley was my grandfather's sister. According to my grandfather's biography, she was born in 1874, which is, auspiciously, exactly one hundred years before my son Ratna Vajra's birth. I remember her funeral vaguely, as if in a dream. I was born in 1945, and my father passed away in 1950, and she passed away before my father passed away. So it must have been in 1947 or 1948.

She was a very great practitioner and master who also went to Kham and traveled in the same area that Tadrin Wangmo did. There were very powerful monasteries from other traditions in that area, and they ruled the region, whereas our Sakya monasteries were small and scattered. She was so great a master that no one called her Jetsunma but instead she was widely known as Kyabgon Pema Trinley. There are many famous incidents related to her life. She was certainly a *yeshé khandroma* (wisdom ḍākinī).

Jamyang Khyentsé Wangpo and Jamgön Kongtrül and Terchen Chokgyur Lingpa had a treasure box that was a round ball with many teachings concealed in it. The prophecy was that to be opened, it required the touch of the blood of a *yeshé khandroma dakpopa* (lineage-owning wisdom ḍākinī). It was in Dergé, and they thought that the blood of one of the queens or princesses of the Dergé line would be able to open it because they were lineage owners, and they waited and got their blood, but it wouldn't open.

But the Sakya are also the lineage owners. Jetsun Pema Trinley's blood was able to open it. She was a very high lama, had many followers, and was a famous teacher, so they were afraid to ask for her blood. But an opportunity arose in Trihor. The Lakasam family, the members of whom were the family of Jamyang Khyentsé Chökyi Lodrö's consort, invited her, and she ate meat with a knife. She was cut by the knife, and they collected her blood in a cloth as they bound it up. They kept the cloth as a very holy thing. When Jamyang Khyentsé Wangpo heard about it, they put the treasure box in the middle and made many offerings around it. They touched it slightly with some of the blood, and it opened immediately. Dezhung Rinpoché told me this story.

She was a disciple of Jamgön Loter Wangpo, and so she received all the initiations of the *Collection of All Tantras*. When she came to Sakya, she usually did retreat. She had done fourteen different retreats. She was a very great practitioner. My sister Jetsun Chimey probably received initiations from her.

One day, Jetsunma was giving initiations in one of the Sakya monasteries. When the monasteries in another tradition heard about this, they were very critical. Firstly, it was because they did not want other traditions to perform initiations without their permission. Secondly, they said that it was very inauspicious for a woman to give initiations. So they sent the *harsh dop dop* (monastic police) to beat her. The dop dop arrived while she was giving an initiation in the temple. As they could not enter straight away, they peeked through the curtains, and Jetsunma saw them. She placed her vase in the space before her, arranged her upper robe, and then again took hold of the vase. They were so astonished that they went in, and instead of beating her, they did prostrations and received blessings from her. Although the only memory of Jetsunma that I have is a vague one of her funeral, my sister on the other hand remembers her very well and has told me innumerable stories about her.

Ane Chime Tenpai Nyima

Ane Chime Tenpai Nyima was a very great Vajrayoginī practitioner. She was my father's sister. She was a very strong practitioner but also very humble. She wouldn't give initiations to anyone but me, and she would always close the door and not let anyone come in. She was too humble to wear the initiation hat. I was given a red hat with a curved top, like khenpos wear, to play with. When I tried to make her wear it during initiation, she refused at first, but finally consented. She passed away due to breast cancer, and she suffered a lot from it. I visited her shortly after I had finished studying the Vajrakīlaya pūjā and sacred dance. She asked me to perform the dance for her, which I did, and she was very impressed. She gave me her *ḍamaru* [a small hand drum] made of ivory with a handle of gold. She asked me to pray for her to be reborn in Khecari. Shortly after that, she passed away.

When her tomb was opened after her cremation, the entire inside was covered with *sindūra* powder, and all of her bones were yellow.

Trinley Paljor Sangmo

My aunt, Trinley Paljor Sangmo, was not a Khön, but she was my father's first wife. My father married her first, but she did not bear him children, so he had to remarry. He chose her sister, my mother, but my mother died soon after my birth. So although my aunt did not give birth to me, she was the one who brought us up, and so ended up being in effect my mother.

She was also a very good practitioner. She barely slept at all—only one or two hours a night—because she was enormously dedicated. She never lay down, but rather sat in a box and ultimately did about six hundred thousand prostrations and made about a million maṇḍala offerings. She also did roughly twenty million guru yogas, although I am uncertain of the exact number. Additionally, she prayed and did sādhanas day and night. She was very, very kind, just like a mother.

Of course, there have been many more female Sakya practitioners, and these I have mentioned are only a few.

Jetsun Kushok Chimey Luding

Reprinted from *Melody of Dharma*, a publication of the office of Sakya Dolma Phodrang.

Her Eminence Jetsun Kushok Chimey Luding is the elder sister of His Holiness Kyabgon Gongma Trichen Rinpoche (the forty-first Sakya Trichen), and one of the greatest female Buddhist masters alive today. She began her religious education when she was five, was ordained as a novice nun at seven, and did her first retreat when she was ten. When His Holiness the Sakya Trichen began his training, Jetsunma was at his side and together they received teachings and empowerments from the greatest teachers of the time, notably Jamyang Khyentsé Chökyi Lodrö, Dampa Rinpoche, and Dezhung Rinpoché, to name but a few. Considered to be an emanation of Vajrayoginī, she is one of the three Sakya women ever to have transmitted the holy Lamdré, which she did for the first time at the age of seventeen.

Throughout her life, Jetsunma had to face many hardships, beginning with the loss of both parents and two siblings when she was still a young child. Exile to India as a nun without the support of a monastery was such a challenge that Jetsunma had no choice but to abandon her robes. When she was twenty-six, she married Rinchen Se Kushok, a brother of Luding Khenchen Rinpoche, head of the Ngor branch of the Sakya school.

When they immigrated to Canada a few years later, they faced the challenge of providing for their young family, and saw themselves forced to work as manual laborers. But Jetsunma remained steadfast, working at a strenuous job, raising her children, and spending entire nights doing her spiritual practice. She slept very little and yet never felt tired.

Their son Luding Khen Rinpoche succeeded his uncle Luding Khenchen Rinpoche as seventy-sixth abbot of the Ngor monastery in Manduwala, and as head of the Ngor branch of the Sakya tradition.

As her children grew, Jetsunma began to teach again, and took on the added responsibility of tending to the spiritual needs of her followers. In addition, Jetsunma founded several Dharma centers, which she visits regularly.

Jetsunma is loved and revered by her large numbers of followers worldwide, for whom her powerful maternal presence is a haven of strength and protection, and her example as an accomplished lay practitioner is a beacon of inspiration.

Part Three

Principles of Tantra

9. Finding the Spiritual Master

Two kinds of beings inhabit this universe: inanimate beings and animate ones. *Inanimate* refers to beings that have no mental feelings, like rivers and mountains and so forth, while *animate* refers to humans and all other beings that have mental feelings. We humans belong to the animate class of beings, and our mental feelings are very powerful. There are many different kinds of human beings in numerous races and various cultures, each with their own views and beliefs, but there is one thing common to all: the wish to be free from suffering and to experience happiness. Furthermore, there is no disagreement to be found on this; everyone agrees on this aim. Regardless of our race, or whether we are believers or nonbelievers, everyone strives to be free from suffering and to attain happiness. Every individual, society, government, and country aims for this.

For the sake of human happiness, humankind has made enormous progress in science and technology. We have gained great benefit from these advances. However, it is quite clear that material progress alone cannot secure for us the true peace and happiness we seek. In order to attain true happiness, it is important that we undergo internal or spiritual development. To attain happiness, it is important that we make both material and spiritual progress.

How then can we progress in the spiritual field? The basis for our spiritual development is our buddha nature. The Buddha said that every sentient being possesses buddha nature. This means that the true nature of our mind is pure—naturally pure—right from the beginning. However, at the moment, we do not see the true nature of our mind, which is covered with delusions and obscurations. These obscurations are not in the nature of the mind. They are only temporary, and we can free ourselves from them. If they were in the nature of the mind, then we would not be able to eliminate them. No matter how much we try to wash coal, for example, it will never become white. Yet with the right remedies, we can remove our mental obscurations. For example, a white cloth covered with dirt will not reveal that it is white until the proper method of washing it with soap and water is applied and all of the dirt is washed away. That is to say, our mind is naturally pure and the obscurations are only temporary. Fortunately, there are methods for eliminating the defilements permanently.

Therefore, if we apply the correct methods and efforts, even as ordinary people, we can eliminate our obscurations and thus realize the true nature of our mind. We can attain the absolute goal, which is real peace and happiness. Even if we do not reach the ultimate realization of our goal, our ongoing efforts to progress spiritually will bring us many benefits, and can give us experiences of deep peace and happiness.

The very first condition that will allow us to grow spiritually is faith; specifically, faith in the teachings. By faith, we do not mean blind faith. Faith means that through our own careful investigations, we come to the irrefutable conclusion that the teachings are genuine. Without this first condition, it is impossible for us to develop any virtuous qualities or to accomplish any virtuous deeds. We are like a roasted seed, unable to sprout even when placed in soil. So too we cannot develop any virtuous qualities without faith.

According to the teachings, there are three kinds of faith: clear faith, aspiring faith, and trusting faith. The first is called "clear faith." When we perceive the great qualities of the Buddha, his teachings, and the community, all of our confusion is cleared and our mind is refreshed. Clear faith is similar in nature to that of a person who, suffering from heat, remembers mountain snow or a cold landscape and so experiences refreshment.

The second kind of faith is called "aspiring faith." At this point, one aspires to achieve spiritual attainment and to acquire virtuous qualities for one's own sake as well as that of others. Just as the only goal of a thirsty elephant in a hot climate is to find water, so our only aspiration is to attain spiritual realization.

Finally, the third kind of faith is called "believing faith" or "trusting faith." This refers to belief in the teachings of the Buddha, particularly in the law of cause and effect, and in the good qualities of the Buddha, Dharma, and Saṅgha. This is like a mother and child who meet after a long separation and still instinctively trust each other.

A human being endowed with these three kinds of faith has developed unshakable faith in the teachings through investigation and analysis, and will not be tempted to forsake the teachings of the Buddha due to the usual causes of abandoning the spiritual path.

There are four causes of abandoning the spiritual path. First, the desire for worldly attainments like wealth or fame can lead us to leave the spiritual path. The second cause is hatred: the rise of anger toward someone can move us to abandon the path. Fear is the third cause of leaving the spiritual path. For example, if remaining on the spiritual path might cause the loss of our lives, this could cause us to abandon the path. The fourth and last cause is ignorance. By this we mean the ignorance of not knowing what to adopt and what to abandon. This lack of clarity takes us away from the spiritual path.

In order to eliminate these four causes of abandoning the spiritual path, we need to fully realize their futility and the harm that they cause us. In the case of the first cause, desire, we need to remember that no matter how much we attain in our worldly lives, or how high a position we reach, this is only temporary and is not really beneficial. There is no comparison to be made between material benefit and spiritual benefit. As for the second cause, hatred, this is the worst defilement that we can harbor. Even merits that have been accumulated over thousands of eons can be lost by giving way to anger even for a single moment. By always remembering the terrible harm that anger can cause, we can eliminate it. Fear, the third cause, can be eradicated by realizing that no matter what harm we face by remaining on the spiritual path—even if it results in the loss of our own life—it can never be as dire as the fall into the lower realms caused by abandonment of the spiritual path. To eliminate the fourth cause, ignorance, we need to always be conscious of what keeps us on the path, and what takes us away from it, and to abide by these criteria. Therefore, the very first thing that we must do on the spiritual path is to establish faith, unshakable faith that will utterly subdue these four causes. This immovable faith will become the basis for all our virtuous qualities.

If we are to embark on the spiritual path, it is equally important and crucial to find a teacher or a spiritual master who can guide us along the way. Even when we undertake an ordinary task, such as acquiring a new skill or going on a journey, the assistance of an experienced guide or teacher is essential. Without this, one can easily learn wrong methods and even go astray. This is particularly relevant in the spiritual field. Knowledge of the spiritual path is not within the reach of ordinary people; it is beyond our comprehension. Therefore, it is imperative that we find the right kind of spiritual guidance when we embark on the spiritual path.

There are different classes of spiritual masters, endowed with varying characteristics and qualifications. We can qualify the masters according to the level of vows that they have taken. There are three such levels of vows. First is the prātimokṣa vow, according to which we pledge to abstain from negative deeds. This vow is taken with a view to our own personal liberation. Second is the bodhisattva vow, which entails not only abstaining from negative deeds but also striving toward liberation for the sake of other beings. Finally, the Vajrayāna or tantric vow is the highest level of vow, and this is where supreme methods are used to gain liberation for the sake of others.

A master who has taken all three of these vows is the highest kind of master that one can find. Finding such a spiritual master is the source of all good qualities, but it is not enough to find this master. We also need to follow his instructions, much like we would a doctor's. In order to recover from an illness, we need to find a good doctor, and we need to follow his advice. Otherwise, even if we have the best doctor possible, we will never recover from our illness. So not only is it vital to find the right spiritual master, but it is equally important that we follow his or her instructions.

When we choose a spiritual master, it is essential that we be very careful. We need to evaluate the master thoroughly before taking him or her as our guide. Even in worldly life, when we undertake something new, we need to evaluate the different ways to proceed. If we are thinking about buying a house, we have to compare different houses, look at the positive and negative attributes of each, and see which one is more advantageous financially, and so forth. Only after such careful investigation can we decide which house to buy. We must utilize the same tools of evaluation when finding a spiritual master.

Of course, compared to buying a house, decisions regarding our spiritual life are far more important. Buying a new house, or anything new, is something that will be part of our lives for a hundred years at best. So if we make a mistake, it will not be harmful for too long a time. But in the spiritual path, if we make a mistake, then not only are we hampered during this lifetime but also for many subsequent lives. Hence, finding the right spiritual path and the right spiritual guide are the most important things that we can do.

In ancient times, there were many teachings in place to guide disciples on how to evaluate teachers and to guide teachers on how to evaluate disciples. Only when both teacher and disciple were satisfied with each other's qualities did they establish a teacher-disciple relationship. This preliminary evaluation is essential, as it can be very dangerous for a teacher and a disciple to establish a relationship before a proper evaluation has been carried out. This is especially important for the disciple, for whom falling into the wrong hands can be a great detriment. Finding the right spiritual master is extremely important.

The teachings state that there are several levels of spiritual masters: superior, inferior, mediocre, and so forth. They classify these levels according to their qualifications. But whatever level a master belongs to, the minimum requirement that he or she should satisfy is that of good discipline or right moral conduct, because moral conduct is the foundation of all good qualities. This moral conduct should not limit itself to appearances but must be genuine.

The second requirement that a teacher should fulfill is that of wisdom acquired from knowledge and from meditation. If a teacher is not endowed with deep-rooted knowledge and understanding of the sūtras and tantras, then that teacher cannot pass them on to his or her disciples.

The third requirement is compassion. The teacher must be motivated by compassion for his or her disciples. The teacher must feel genuine desire for them to become free from ignorance, to abstain from negative deeds, and to practice virtuous deeds.

In this dark age, it is difficult to find the perfect teacher. However, a teacher who does actualize these three requirements, whose moral qualities are highly developed and whose faults are minimal, qualifies as suitable.

Especially in the Vajrayāna teachings, the teacher is absolutely essential. Trying to learn tantra on our own or through books can actually cause more harm than benefit. Vajrayāna is the most advanced teaching of the Buddha, and it can only be received through the direct transmission of an unbroken lineage that originated with Buddha Vajradhara and has been passed on from one master to another until the present. It is not only the words and their meanings that are conveyed in the teachings. More importantly, it is the blessing that is transmitted from one person to another. Without this blessing, it is impossible to practice any of the tantric teachings or to attain any of their results. It can, in fact, be very harmful. This is why Vajrayāna teachings place so much importance on the spiritual master.

The sun shines brightly in the sky every day, but if we want to channel and maximize its energy, we need certain instruments. Similarly, the blessings of the Buddha shower on sentient beings all the time. But, without proper instruments, we cannot receive these blessings. Due to the lack of merit brought about by our negative deeds, we cannot see the Buddha in person. The guru is the instrument that helps channel and maximize the Buddha's blessings. The guru appears to us in ordinary form, and through him or her, we can hear the teachings of the Buddha and thereby receive his blessings.

Again, it is extremely important in Vajrayāna to find a teacher and to thoroughly investigate his or her qualities. Once we are convinced that the person is a genuine spiritual master, then we can take him or her as our teacher and receive Vajrayāna teachings and initiations from that one. Once we have established a master-disciple relationship with a teacher, we should never break our bond with our teacher and we should never abandon our faith in them no matter what circumstances may arise. Even if we see faults in our master, we should never see these as his or her faults. Any faults we see in the guru, we should see as our own faults. It is much like the moon's reflection on water: if the water is clear, the reflection of the moon is also clear. If the water is muddy, then the moon's reflection is blurred. If, due to our obscurations, we find fault with the master, we should always remember to look at this as our own shortcoming, our own fault, not that of the master.

There are many wonderful stories about ancient Indian masters. These great mahāsiddhas often displayed outlandish behavior and did weird things—very weird things. The disciples who lost faith in their master did not progress on the spiritual path, while those who did not lose their faith in their master experienced spiritual attainment.

There is much talk about root lamas. According to the Vajrayāna teachings, a root lama or guru is someone who bestows the major initiations on us, as well as the tantric teachings and pith instructions. This is our root guru. In actuality, we can have several root gurus. Then, among these, we can also have a very special root guru—for instance, our karmic-link guru. This is our most important guru, someone with whom we have a karmic connection or who has been our guide through the course of many lifetimes. If we have such a guru, it is essential that we never cease to feel intense devotion for them and that we never lose faith in them, whatever happens. Even if our root guru is just an ordinary person and not a realized being, if we as a disciple see that one as the Buddha, then we can receive the blessings of the Buddha, because both the guru and we are endowed with buddha nature.

As explained, it is very important in the Vajrayāna or tantric teachings to find the right guru and, after finding him or her, to establish a strong karmic connection. Without this, it is impossible to make any spiritual progress. It is clearly mentioned in the teachings that it can be very dangerous to practice tantra on our own without depending on a spiritual master who can bestow upon us the unbroken transmission of blessings. Lack of a teacher can cause us to fall into the lower realms. In every tradition, finding the spiritual master and following him or her in the right way is the source of all good qualities. This is particularly true in the Vajrayāna path, where the unbroken lineage of transmission from the Buddha Vajradhara to us is an essential practice. The spiritual master who gives us this transmission is the one who clears away all of our obscurations and confusion and who leads us on the path to liberation. I pray that everyone finds the right spiritual master and successfully establishes the karmic links with him or her that allow the disciple to receive all the blessings of the Buddha.

10. Essence of Tantra

In his infinite compassion, wisdom, and power, the Lord Buddha Śākyamuni gave innumerable teachings aimed at helping countless beings with their infinitely diverse dispositions. These teachings can be classified according to two approaches: Śrāvakayānaand Mahāyāna. Śrāvakayāna is sometimes also called Hīnayāna, and is mainly aimed at individual salvation, while Mahāyāna stresses the universal ideal of the bodhisattva. Mahāyāna itself may be further divided into (1) the Pāramitāyāna, or Perfection Vehicle, also known as Cause Vehicle—according to which the bodhisattva cultivates moral perfection as a cause for future buddhahood—and (2) the Mantrayāna, or Mantra Vehicle, also known as Result Vehicle—whereby one realizes wisdom or gnosis through following certain practices. While both vehicles were practiced widely in Tibet, Mantrayāna and its four classes of tantra—kriyā, caryā, yoga, and anuttarayoga—were especially prized. They were seen as a precious jewel whose purity was preserved through the development of a cohesive monastic tradition and isolated from the external world.

The word *tantra* is seldom used in Tibetan Buddhism, and usually refers to the body of tantric scriptures. The terms *Mantrayāna* or *Vajrayāna* are more commonly used in reference to a doctrinal system. The term *Vajrayāna* refers to the spiritual path that is immutable—the Diamond Vehicle that leads to the realization of the enlightenment mind and that is ever present, although currently obscured by our ignorance. Etymologically, the word *tantra* may be understood as a continuum, a thread or lineage that gives continuity to the teachings, much like the genetic code that determines the form insects, birds, and all sentient creatures take at birth. So tantra, in the Buddhist sense, may be understood as that genetic code that links our buddha nature through successive incarnations until enlightenment is attained. And so a Vajrayāna initiation in one lifetime may result in a rebirth as a Buddhist or as one who embarks on the bodhisattva path.

The tantras are sacred texts that have no temporal beginning. They do not originate in the human realm. Buddhist and Hindu tantras share many similarities but also have many differences. The tantras propounded by Śākyamuni Buddha, such as the *Hevajra Tantra*, the *Kālacakra Tantra*, and the *Guhyasamāja Tantra*, find their origin in words revealed to him by Ādibuddha Vajradhara. It is through the practice of these tantras that the Buddha attained enlightenment.

Although tantrism is a method common to both Hinduism and Buddhism, there are many differences in substance and detail between the two. The complementary character of Buddhist and Hindu tantras developed as alternative ways to seek release from the bondage of saṃsāra. There is some speculation that tantrism goes back to the pre-Aryan era, to the earliest known phase of Indian civilization. Scholars believe that it originated in northwest India, and that it spread through the Himalayan foothills to the entire Indian subcontinent. Many of the tantric deities began as local gods and goddesses that were incorporated into the tantric system. The system was widely practiced by both religions in the fourth and fifth centuries C.E. and reached its peak in India in the tenth and eleventh centuries.

According to some Tibetan and Indian scholars, several of the eighty-four Buddhist mahāsiddhas (greatly realized yogis) were actually Hindu mahāsiddhas. A case in point would be the great Buddhist mahāsiddha Luipa, whom some sources quote as being the Hindu mahāsiddha Matsyendranātha. These "perfected ones" were collectively known in Indian and Tibetan histories as the eighty-four siddhas. It is to their biographies that we must turn if we are to understand the oral transmission of the earliest tantras.

Tantra is a method, a technique. Its earliest practitioners were not interested in labels, any more that a nuclear physicist cares about his nationality when he compares notes with a foreign colleague. They were concerned with method and debated the efficacy of their respective techniques. Many

Hindu practitioners were eventually persuaded to adopt the Mahāyāna view.

There were many schools of Hindu tantrism in ancient India, wherein philosophical views differed widely, ranging all the way from nihilism to materialism. Here, however, the word *tantra* may be understood in the Hindu sense of interwovenness, much as the threads of a fabric are metaphors for the complementary union of the male and female principles of cosmic passivity and power.

We are not well versed in Hindu tantrism and can only speak with authority about our own tradition. Buddhist and Hindu tantras share a similar technology in which there is an orderly structure that is in keeping with the esoteric connective tissue of macrocosm and microcosm. But although they share a methodology, Hindu and Buddhist tantras differ radically in their philosophies.

In Hindu tantra, the focus is placed on the female Śakti as the spiritual basis of our world, which is her manifestation. Liberation means casting off the limitations set by human birth. The self's ultimate union with God or Brahman may be attained during mortal life by means of the body, when the internal Śakti reaches union with the internal Śiva. Liberation arises from the merging of the inner universal principle (*ātman*) with the external principle (*brahman*). The identity of the self or the individual soul (*jīva*) with the absolute is a tenet of Vedic and Hindu belief. Brahman is considered to be a self-existent entity, an eternal unchanging essence of reality.

On the other hand, we find that in the Buddhist tantras, the consort is referred to as *prajñā*, or insight or wisdom. The terms *yoginī* (female yogic practitioner), *vidyā* (knowledge), *mudrā* (seal), and *devī* (goddess) refer to the female principle. The goddess as the Perfection of Wisdom (*prajñāpāramitā*) appears as the final truth of emptiness (*śūnyatā*).

Omniscient knowledge has compassion (*karuṇā*) as its root. It has the enlightenment mind as its nature. It has the vow of the bodhisattva as its motivation, and it contains the means for the result. The two—wisdom and compassion—are identified with the perfections of the bodhisattva and the intermingling of nirvāṇa and saṃsāra, so that when this wisdom is combined with means or method, it is no longer passive but appears in its fully active form. As Lord Buddha Śākyamuni was a *kṣatriya* (military ruling caste), some of the rituals of the Buddhist tantras may be traced back to the old Vedic rituals, such as the fire ritual, and to the Upaniṣads.

But again, while the practices may be similar in form, the philosophies behind them vary radically. Buddhists see reality as having no ultimate self-existence and no true self-nature. The three kāyas of a buddha are associated with the spiritual and external spheres of the cosmological map and also with certain places in the human body. We meditate on the heavenly and earthly divinities within the body, but the most important thing is that we take the generation of the enlightenment mind as the very foundation of our practice.

In all the Mahāyāna schools, enlightenment mind is the root cause for the spiritual path. The human body contains the nature of the dharmakāya, saṃbhogakāya, and the nirmāṇakāya as the three bodies of our enlightened buddha nature, but without the generation of enlightenment thought, no result can arise. These are some of the essential differences between the Buddhist and Hindu views.

In the Buddhist tantras, the union of prajñā and karuṇā, insight and compassion, produces the fullness of cosmic awareness through the meeting of opposites. It is central to the notion of sacred and profane when these are viewed in the mirror of the clear light of mind itself.

The mind has many facets. Its foundation is the all-base consciousness, which is called *kunshi* in Tibetan or *ālaya* in Sanskrit. This is the basis upon which both saṃsāra and nirvāṇa are built. It is the clear aspect of mind itself. It does not focus on other things but rests in perception of itself, as it has done from beginningless time and will do until enlightenment is reached.

Mahāyānists believe that we should enter neither saṃsāra nor nirvāṇa, but that we should follow the middle path. Through the power of our wisdom, we do not remain in saṃsāra, and through the power of our compassion, we do not remain in nirvāṇa. When we attain enlightenment, which we call nonabiding nirvāṇa, we are free from suffering but we remain in saṃsāra out of compassion for beings who are trapped in it, and we help them.

In Buddhist metaphysics, the philosophical view of emptiness, or *śūnyatā*, is paramount to achieving liberation. If we realize that reality has no ultimate self-existence and that all appearances arise from the mind, we attain the view of the nonduality of saṃsāra and nirvāṇa. We clearly see that saṃsāra is nirvāṇa, and we enter into direct contact with our buddha nature, and enlightenment becomes within reach in this very lifetime.

Vajrayāna is a method. Its primary intention and its final goal are the same as those of the Mahāyāna, but it provides a methodology of far greater efficacy in that it calls for us to use both our mind and body in its practice. It is the most sophisticated technology available for attaining liberation. It is a bit like traveling by airplane rather than by train. An airplane needs many conditions in order to fly: fuel, air, a reliable engine, an efficient design, and so forth. Likewise, when we seek realization through Vajrayāna we need to exert ourselves assiduously to fulfill all of the necessary requisites for the attainment of the result. Preeminent among these requisites is our personal, daily meditation on the two stages of creation and completion and the visualization of the maṇḍala and the deity. The recitation of mantras, the practice of physical yogas such as the breathing yoga, the yoga of inner heat, the dream yoga and meditative postures, the nurturing of the enlightenment mind, and the cultivation of ethical conduct are also crucial factors.

After we receive a Vajrayāna initiation, there are many vows to be kept in addition to both the monastic prātimokṣa vows and the Mahāyāna vows. There are also tantric vows, without which no practice can be effective. It is much like a farmer looking after his crops. If he is to have the right conditions for a good harvest, he must protect his crop from adverse elements like hailstorms or floods. He must ensure that the soil is properly fertilized and he must provide it with sufficient sunlight and water, and so forth. In the same way, when we seek spiritual results, we need to set the right conditions. If we practice correctly, then the attainment of the view of the nondifferentiation of saṃsāra and nirvāṇa will naturally arise, and with it the mundane and supramundane siddhis that enable us to help other beings.

The tantric method used in Tibet was very sophisticated and carefully systematized so that sincere and able practitioners were guaranteed results, provided they had the enlightenment mind as their root motivation. As was mentioned earlier, generation of the enlightenment mind is central to both Mahāyāna and Vajrayāna practice. The three foundations are loving-kindness, compassion, and the generation of enlightenment mind (bodhicitta). All practice must arise from selflessness. Loving-kindness means that we want all beings in all realms of existence to be happy; compassion is the wish that sentient beings should be free from suffering; and the generation of the enlightenment mind is the pursuit of enlightenment for the sake of all sentient beings. Without love and compassion, the enlightenment mind will not arise. Without the enlightenment mind, liberation cannot be attained. If the enlightenment mind is like a seed that we plant, love and compassion are like the water that we pour on it while it grows to fruition.

Candrakīrti wrote in the *Madhyamakāvatāra* that the śrāvakas and pratyekabuddhas are born of buddhas, while buddhas are born of the bodhisattvas, and bodhisattvas are born of love and compassion—especially from compassion. Thus he paid special homage to compassion, without which the root cause of enlightenment cannot arise. This, then, is why we meditate on some father and mother tantras, wherein the deities are in union, the union of wisdom and compassion.

During the period of Buddhism's greatest flowering in ancient India, there was a vast tantric tradition related to the practice of the maṇḍala. The term *mantra* may be defined as a method for protecting the mind against conceptualization, or concepts that possess certain marks or characteristics. The efficacy of Vajrayāna rests upon many factors, the most important one of which is the line of direct transmission of initiation (*abhiṣeka*), which has been unbroken since the Lord Śākyamuni Buddha set into motion the wheel of Dharma. The term *maṇḍala* may be briefly defined as a method by which one can reach and maintain the spontaneous coemergent wisdom of great bliss that is always present within the mind. In order to enter into the practice of the maṇḍala, one must receive an initiation, a consecration.

Transmission is particularly important in Vajrayāna, as the guru is part of a lineage of teachers who have received direct transmission originating from the Ādibuddha Vajradhara, the Buddha under whom all the five Buddha families can be subsumed. This direct unbroken blessing must be received before the special ripening can occur. It is said in the tantras that, if we wish to receive a transmission, we need to find the guru with whom we have a special karmic connection, and who has all the qualifications to teach the tantras. When we find this guru, we should receive transmissions and explanations from that one.

The guru is a master who confers upon us initiation into the mysteries of religion. The efficacy of initiation is that it purifies appearances relating to the defilements that hinder the essential nature of great bliss that resides in the mind. It has the capacity for that awakening that makes one a fit vessel for contemplating the clear light. The continuity of the Vajrayāna initiation has been maintained through an unbroken transmission that serves to mature the practitioner and lead him or her to liberation.

We must receive the teaching on the five Buddha families in the form of a *wang kurwa* (*dbang bskur ba*), or empowerment, the transmission or permission to practice tantra. After receiving the transmission, we must fulfill its obligations and learn to see ourselves very clearly as the result. Then, because of the special connection between cause and result, the result will naturally arise. A major empowerment is never given to a person who does not have the capacity to generate the enlightenment mind.

If, in Mahāyāna, one must not practice without a teacher, this is all the more true of Vajrayāna. In this day and age, most teachings are written down; nevertheless, they must always be taught orally. One cannot attain any result by merely studying a text. In Vajrayāna, it is necessary to receive the *wang kurwa*, which is the door to tantra, and without which one cannot undertake its practice. In many cases, a clear sign appears when we find the guru with whom we have a karmic link. The moment the great Sakya teacher Tsarchen heard of the Sakya teacher Doringpa, he felt an immediate and compelling urge to meet him then and there. Vajrayoginī, the female deity, appeared to him and gave him a book saying, "This book was sent to you by Doringpa." Tsarchen then asked around to find where Doringpa was and made the effort to meet him. When he received the consecration and instructions from him, he achieved far greater results than ever before. Generally speaking, there is an unmistakable sign that indicates when we have found our guru.

Mahāyāna is referred to as the causal path, or causal yāna, because within it we strive to practice moral conduct in order the create the right causes for liberation. Vajrayāna is called the result yāna, because from the beginning we visualize ourselves as the Buddha in one form or another. By practicing visualization in this way, the immense qualities of the Buddha will automatically arise in our being. Our entire organism actually is the pure Buddha and always has been, but because we are wrapped in illusion, we are not able to see it.

This is not an arbitrary conclusion. We have the example of countless others who have purified their obscurations and achieved enlightenment using these methods. There are many tendencies or predispositions that need to be transformed because they are the cause of much suffering. These have no base in the ālaya, or base consciousness—consequently they can be the cause of much suffering. We can take as an example the transformation of sexual energies; they are conventionally regarded as hindrances to the spiritual path, but if correctly used, they can help us immensely. In fact, there is no such thing as impurity. Impurities appear because we have not realized the true nature of our mind and we are still thinking in terms of subject and object.

There are infinite numbers of buddhas of all types, but they can be divided into five categories, which represent the five qualities of the Buddha. Although these five can be included in the single one, the teachings of the five different types of buddhas provide a basis from which to begin. We imagine a maṇḍala that contains the five Dhyani Buddhas, all of whom have attained enlightenment as Buddha Śākyamuni did, in one eon or another. Four of them are placed at the four cardinal points and one is placed at the center of the maṇḍala. The Buddha at the center is dark blue and is called Akṣobhya, or the Unmoving One. In the east is the white Buddha Vairocana, the One Who Creates Appearances. In the south is yellow Ratnasaṃbhava, the One Who Has the Nature of a Gem, and in the west is red Amitābha, which means Limitless Light. In the north is green Amoghasiddhi, the One Who Is Skilled in Accomplishing All Possible Acts.

They are all in the form of Buddha Śākyamuni, except that they have different hand gestures. Akṣobhya displays the *bhūmisparśa mudrā*, or earth-touching gesture, while Vairocana's hands are in the gesture of teaching. Ratnasaṃbhava displays the gesture of giving; Amitābha, the gesture of meditation; and Amoghasiddhi holds up his right hand to show the crossed vajra on his palm, the gesture of fearlessness.

These five deities and their colors are related to the five most common defilements that we are afflicted with as a result of the obscurations of our human condition: blue Akṣobhya is related to anger, white Vairocana to ignorance, yellow Ratnasaṃbhava to pride and miserliness, red Amitābha to desire, and green Amoghasiddhi to envy. There are also marks of the five Buddha races on the bodies of beings. Persons who are often angry will have a mark similar to a vajra on their body, and they can clearly be recognized as belonging to the Vajra family of Akṣobhya. Since the Buddha Akṣobhya represents the complete transformation of anger, these persons will succeed with particular ease and swiftness in purifying their defilements if they practice the path related to Akṣobhya. In the Vajrayāna, we never regard any particular defilement such as anger or desire as something to be repressed, but rather we see the energies tied up in the defilements as material to be purified and transformed into the five Buddhas, each of whom is the embodiment of a particular aspect of wisdom.

This is another reason why we call Vajrayāna the result path. There are limitless beings with different tastes and predispositions. People with strong desire meditate on deities in a passionate form, embracing consorts surrounded by many goddesses. For people with much hatred, there are meditations on deities in very wrathful forms. Those with much ignorance can meditate on very elaborate deities with many jewels and ornaments. Actually, these are all different aspects of the same transcendental wisdom.

Transcendental wisdom is divine wisdom, the power and energy of the Buddha. Many of the tantras were given by Lord Buddha Śākyamuni, including the *Hevajra Tantra*, upon which the main Sakya practice of Lamdré is founded. This is an extensive teaching incorporating all the practices of Theravāda, Mahāyāna, and Vajrayāna. In our tradition, it was transmitted directly by Hevajra's consort Nairātmyā to Virūpa, the great Indian mahāsiddha and sage from Nālandā, and was later brought to Tibet by the translator Drokmi, who lived between 992 and 1072 C.E.

The Lamdré, or "Path as Result," is a vast teaching based on the empowerment and practice of the *Hevajra Tantra*. It includes the philosophy of tantra as well as all of the tantric practices—such as the yoga of inner heat, the yoga of dreams, breathing practices, and so forth. Many other traditions of tantra practiced by mahāsiddhas and pandits of ancient India have specific transmissions that were introduced into Tibet by the translators and have been upheld to the present day.

One such transmission is the Vajramālā, or Vajra Rosary, which came from the great Indian master Abhayākaragupta, who was blessed by a vision of the deity Vajrayoginī on three occasions. Abhayākaragupta was a great pandit endowed with the highest capabilities. He had seen the nature of reality, he had received direct inspiration from the deity, and he was immensely learned. It is on the basis of these criteria that he composed the collection of scriptures known as the Vajramālā. Avalokiteśvara conferred many outer, inner, and secret teachings upon him. These teachings served as the basis upon which Abhayākaragupta composed treatises relating to nearly two hundred different maṇḍalas. These have come down to us to the present day without any break in their transmission. There are also many special esoteric teachings, such as those of Nāropa on the *Eleven Yogas of Vajrayoginī*, those of Mahākāla, and especially those of Vajrakīlaya from the old Nyingmapa tradition, which our family still upholds. There is also Sarvavid, which is used for the dying and the dead; Vajrabhairava, the wrathful form of Mañjuśrī from the Golden Dharmas; and many others. But most of the basic Sakya teachings from the preparation stage to the attainment of enlightenment are included in the Lamdré. Other transmissions including the collections of Abhayākaragupta and Mitrayogin can be found in the *Collection of All Tantras* (*Rgyud sde kun btus*), which, in addition to those already mentioned, includes collections from other traditions.

As the tantras were in danger of being lost, the publication of the compendium of the *Collection of All Tantras* was initiated in the nineteenth century by Jamyang Loter Wangpo. He supervised the preparation of thirty-two volumes, which were the result of centuries of meticulous collecting by encyclopedists. He himself was considered to be an emanation of Vajrapāṇi, the Lord of Secrets, who held and protected the teachings of Śākyamuni, and he is said to have been the one who gathered and preserved essential teachings in this degenerate age. Jamyang Loter Wangpo's qualities and learning were inconceivably vast.

Why do we find liberation through the practice of Vajrayāna? The motivation with which Lord Buddha taught us to pursue the bodhisattva ideal is the cause that actually takes us to liberation, and the continuity of its blessing has never been interrupted since the Ādibuddha Vajradhara down to the present day. A succession of teachers have scrupulously maintained the purity of the Lord Buddha's essential teaching on the nondifferentiation of saṃsāra and nirvāṇa and have made available to others an immense variety of methods to help beings with different personalities gain realization. As they were themselves intent on enlightenment, their blessings have resulted in a rain of wisdom for those who pursue the bodhisattva ideal.

11. Process of Tantra

Embarking on the Tantric Path

The tantric path begins as the Buddhist path. There is no important philosophical difference between tantric Buddhism and Mahāyāna Buddhism—the difference is one of emphasis and method. Let us first look at the practical beginning of the tantric path. It is said that the tantric path begins as the Buddhist path, so it is not surprising that the first step on the tantric path is the taking of refuge. In the Tibetan tantric tradition, refuge is taken with a qualified guru who represents a recognized spiritual lineage. In a sense, the act of taking refuge is an initiation. First and foremost it represents an initiation into the Buddhist religion, and it is the first step that we take on the Buddhist path to liberation.

The reasons for taking refuge in the Triple Gem are three: fear, faith, and compassion. Fear, in the sense that we take refuge in the Triple Gem out of fear of the suffering of saṃsāra; faith, meaning that we believe that only the Triple Gem has the power to relieve us from the suffering of saṃsāra; and compassion, because, just as we fear the suffering of saṃsāra, so do all other living beings. And so we take refuge in the Triple Gem for the sake of all living beings.

The next step on the tantric path is the production of enlightenment thought (*bodhicitta*), which is the resolution to attain enlightenment for the sake of all beings. The creation of enlightenment thought is closely connected to the vows of the bodhisattva. In brief, the essence of the bodhisattva's practice is the altruistic wish to benefit all living beings. Like the taking of refuge, the creation of enlightenment thought is a necessary preliminary to the practice of the tantric path.

The next step is to reflect on death, impermanence, and the human condition. We should recognize that the happiness and favorable circumstances that we enjoy at the present moment are not permanent. These will all disappear at the time of death and, moreover, there is no certainty as to when death will occur. Reflecting on death and impermanence encourages us to practice the Dharma without delay.

Next, we should understand the law of karma, or the law of cause and effect, and its relation to our actions. We should come to realize that good actions such as generosity and compassion are the cause of happiness, while unwholesome actions like selfishness and hatred are the cause of suffering. As there is no way to avoid the good or bad results of actions, we should strive to do only good actions and to avoid unwholesome ones.

In the Tibetan tantric tradition, certain preliminary practices are usually performed before entering the tantric path itself. There are four main preliminary practices. The first is the recitation of the refuge prayer one hundred thousand times. The second is the recitation of the one-hundred-syllable Vajrasattva mantra one hundred thousand times. The third is the recitation of a prayer to the guru one hundred thousand times. The last is performing one hundred thousand maṇḍala offerings, by which one symbolically offers the entire universe for the sake of one's spiritual progress.

The first part of the preliminary practices serves to set us firmly on the Buddhist path. The second is meant to purify us of past and present negative tendencies. The third establishes a strong bond between ourselves and our guru, while the last helps to rid us of selfish tendencies through the symbolic act of giving, while enabling us to accumulate the merit necessary to be successful on the path. After completing all these preliminaries, we ask the guru for initiation into the meditational practices associated with one of the tantric tutelary deities, which are emanations of the Buddha. Initiation into these practices must be given by a qualified guru who represents a recognized spiritual lineage. Tantric initiation enables us to visualize and identify ourselves with the purified universe of the tutelary deity, the symbolic representation of the enlightened experience.

The similarity that is seen to exist between Hindu and Buddhist tantra has occasionally led some to assume that what originally distinguished Buddhist philosophy from its Hindu counterpart was forsaken with the development of tantra. This, however, is not true, because tantra is concerned with the means of achieving spiritual progress, not with philosophy. So the similarity between Hindu and Buddhist tantric practices is not an indication of Hindu and Buddhist philosophies merging. The fact, for example, that a number of terms and deities are shared by Hindu and Buddhist tantra does not mean that tantric Buddhism has strayed from the essence of Buddhist thought. For instance, although a number of terms like *svabhāva* and *ātman* that are commonly found in Hinduism also occur in Buddhist tantric writings, they do not have the same meaning. The term *svabhāva,* which in Hinduism means "the existence of an independent nature," is used in Buddhist tantra to emphasize the emptiness of all things. Thus it is said that the nature of all things is emptiness. Similarly, the term *ātman*, or "self," is merely used to identify one with emptiness.

The fact that several deities are worshiped by both Hindus and Buddhists does not mean that Buddhist philosophy has lost its distinctive character. In the first place, the Hindu deities included in the Buddhist tantric pantheon are deities of lesser importance. Secondly, since both Buddhism and Hinduism developed within the Indian cultural context, it is not surprising that a number of deities should be adopted by both traditions. Such deities are in themselves neither Buddhist nor Hindu; they simply belong to Indian culture. In short, tantra is concerned with methodology more than with philosophy. Not only Buddhist and Hindu but Jain and even Islamic tantric practices show many similarities. Despite the similarities between Buddhist and Hindu tantric practices, tantric Buddhism has always retained its own philosophical view.

It was mentioned above that there is no important philosophical difference between tantric Buddhism and Mahāyāna Buddhism. Mahāyāna Buddhism contains two principal philosophical schools—that of mind, the Mind-Only school, and that of emptiness, the Madhyamaka school. These schools were explained at length by Asaṅga and Nāgārjuna, respectively, who are recognized by the Tibetan tantric tradition as the fathers of Buddhist tantra as we know it. And hence, there are two chief elements in Buddhist tantric philosophy—mind and emptiness. The focus on the importance of mind is the starting point of tantric Buddhist philosophy. Mind is the first step in the process of gaining freedom, not the last, because in order to gain freedom, one must also understand emptiness.

The process of gaining freedom by understanding emptiness is explained in the Tibetan tantric tradition by means of four steps illustrated by examples. The first step expresses the idea that our situation is dependent upon our mind. When, for instance, someone has taken alcohol, he may feel that the ground is moving or that he has great strength. Again, one who is suffering from jaundice perceives white objects as yellow. These examples show that our perceptions are conditioned by the state of our mind. The second stage is illustrated by the example of a magical illusion. The point here is that although perceptions depend upon mind, mind itself is illusory. Mind, in fact, is nothing itself. It is neither within nor without, neither long nor short. Just as when a magical apparatus is assembled, the magical illusion appears, and when the apparatus is not assembled, the illusion does not appear, so all experience is like a magical illusion.

The third step is to understand all things as interdependently originated. This is also illustrated by means of examples. For instance, if a number of vessels filled with clear water are placed outside on a moonlit and cloudless night, the moon's reflection will appear in the vessels of water. If any of the conditions such as cloudlessness are missing, the moon's reflection will not appear. In the same way, all things appear as the result of a combination of conditions—that is, they are interdependently originated.

Finally, all things are understood to be inexpressible. This is shown by means of examples like the following: although a sprout is produced from a seed, it cannot be said that the sprout and the seed are identical, nor can it be said that they are different. So the relationship between the seed and the sprout is inexpressible. So it is that all things that are interdependently originated are inexpressible in the ultimate sense.

These four steps of Buddhist tantric theory, illustrated in the foregoing examples, show how the ideas of mind and emptiness work together. The first step calls for seeing all things as dependent upon mind, and the next three steps call for seeing all things as similar to a magical illusion:

interdependently originated and inexpressible—in other words, empty. So here, mind is the key to changing our way of seeing things.

Mind is responsible for the experience of saṃsāra and nirvāṇa. But mind is nothing itself; it is empty. If mind had a nature of its own, it would always create either saṃsāra or nirvāṇa according to its nature, but mind is like a crystal or a white cloth. If we place a crystal next to a blue or red object, the crystal will appear blue or red accordingly. If we dye a cloth red or blue, it will turn red or blue accordingly. So too with the mind. If it is conditioned by attachment, aversion, and ignorance, it appears as saṃsāra, but if it is conditioned by enlightenment, it appears as nirvāṇa, the experience of a buddha.

It is said that the practice of tantra can speed up the process of gaining liberation or enlightenment. Why should this be so? It is because tantra provides more efficient means of changing ordinary experience into enlightened experience. The key to the accelerating effect of tantric practices is the fact that tantra employs a variety of powerful psychophysical forces, which it deliberately manipulates in order to achieve more rapid results. This enables one who practices tantra to achieve quickly—even in a single lifetime—a level of spiritual maturity that it would otherwise take many lifetimes to realize.

Whoever practices tantra is concerned with the control and manipulation of psychological and physical energy. He or she seeks to direct that energy toward attaining the goal of enlightenment. The energy is in itself pure since it shares the nature of all things, which is emptiness. Quantitatively, the energy produced from powerful emotions like desire and anger far outweighs that produced from milder emotions. If properly used, these powerful forces may be transformed in such a way as to contribute to our progress toward the goal of attaining enlightenment.

Tantra turns the energy of the defilements—desire and hatred—into the means of liberation. Tantra is like a kind of spiritual judo in which the strength of one's enemy is used to gain victory over him. Although it is said that tantra provides a means of achieving rapid spiritual progress, this does not mean that tantra is an easy path. It requires strict adherence to the rules of good conduct and a sincere and dedicated approach to the practice of the spiritual path. If you bring these qualities to the practice of tantra, then your swift progress toward the goal of enlightenment is assured.

Comparison of Tantra to Other Buddhist Schools

There is a common misconception among many non-Buddhists (and even among certain Buddhists) that the tantras are late and corrupt additions to the Buddha's teachings. This is false. The tantras are the genuine teachings of Lord Buddha, and they occupy a paramount position within the overall framework of the Buddhist doctrine. Some of the misconceptions about the tantras stem from their esoteric nature. Since the time of the Buddha, the tantras were always taught secretly and selectively. For their correct understanding, they have always required the oral instructions of a qualified master; without such explanations, they can easily be misunderstood in wrong and harmful ways. As a follower of this tradition, I too am prevented from discussing most aspects of tantra here. But it is perhaps permissible in these circumstances to say a few general things about Buddhist thought and practice. For this, I shall base myself on the teachings of our tradition, such as in the *General System of the Tantras* by Lopön Sönam Tsemo.

In the Tibetan tradition, the word *tantra* (*rgyud*) normally refers to a special class of the Buddha's teachings and to the scriptures that embody it. But contrary to its English usage, the word does not usually refer to the whole system of tantric practice and theory. For the doctrinal system of tantra, the terms *Mantrayāna* and *Vajrayāna* (the Vajra or Adamantine Vehicle) are used instead. In its technical sense, the word *tantra* means continuum. In particular, tantra refers to one's own mind as nondual wisdom. There exists a continuum in that there is an unbroken continuation of mind from beginningless time until the attainment of buddhahood.

This mental continuum, moreover, has three aspects or stages. These are the causal continuum, the continuum involved in applied method, and the result continuum. Sentient creatures in ordinary cyclic existence are the causal continuum. Those who have engaged in the methods of gaining liberation are the method continuum. And those who have achieved the ultimate spiritual fruit, the body of wisdom, are the result continuum. The causal continuum is so called because there exists in it the potential for producing a fruit if the right conditions are met, even though at present that fruit is not actually manifested. It is like a seed kept in a container. The method continuum is so called because there exist means or methods by which the result, which is latent in the cause, can be produced. Method is like the water and fertilizer needed for growing a plant. The fruit, or result, refers to the actualization of the result that was latent in the cause. This is like the ripened flower that blooms when one has planted the seed and properly cultivated the plant.

As we've discussed, Mahāyāna can be divided into two: Pāramitāyāna, or Perfection Vehicle, and Mantrayāna, or Secret Mantra Vehicle. The spiritual fruit or goal of both branches of Mahāyāna practice is the perfect awakening or enlightenment of buddhahood. A perfectly awakened buddha is one who has correctly understood the status of all knowable things in ultimate reality, who possesses consummate bliss that is free from the impurities, and who has eliminated all stains of obscurations. The latter characteristic, freedom from obscurations, is a cause for other features of buddhahood. It consists of the elimination of the three types of defilements: defilements such as hatred and desire, defilements that obstruct one's knowledge of reality as it is in its multiplicity, and defilements that pertain to the meditative attainments.

We speak of a method of spiritual practice as a path because it is a means by which one reaches the spiritual goal one is aiming for. There are two types of paths. One is the common path that leads to inferior results, and the other is the extraordinary path that leads to the highest goal. Some religious or philosophical traditions, while claiming to yield good results, actually lead their practitioners to undesirable destinations. For instance, the inferior *tīrthikas* (of certain non-Buddhist Indian schools), as well as those who propound nihilism, only lead their followers to rebirths in the miserable realms of existence. The higher tīrthikas can lead to the acquisition of a rebirth in the higher realms, but not to liberation. And even the paths of the śrāvakas and pratyekabuddhas are inferior, for they lead only to simple liberation and not to complete buddhahood.

The first major division of Mahāyāna, the Perfection Vehicle, is also considered general Mahāyāna, because it is held in common with both Mahāyāna divisions, whereas the second is termed particular Mahāyāna, because its profound and vast doctrine is not found within the general tradition. One essential difference between the two Mahāyāna approaches can be explained by way of their approach to the sensory objects that are the basis for both cyclic existence and nirvāṇa. In the Perfection Vehicle, one tries to banish the five classes of sensory objects outright. One first restrains oneself physically and verbally from overt misdeeds related to the objects of sense desire, and then by studying and reasoning, one learns about their nature. Afterward, through meditative realization, one removes all attachment to them. This is done on two levels. On the relative level, one removes attachment through cultivating the antidote to the defilements by means of meditation, such as by cultivating love as the antidote to anger, and a view of the repulsiveness of the sense objects as the antidote to desire. And on the ultimate level, attachment is removed through understanding and meditatively realizing that all of these objects in fact are without any independent self-nature.

In the Secret Mantra Vehicle, one also begins by restraining oneself outwardly (the essential basis for one's conduct is the morality of the prātimokṣa and bodhisattva vows). However, in one's attitude toward the sense objects, one does not try to eliminate them directly. Some will of course argue that such objects of sensory desire can only act as fetters that prevent one's liberation, and that they must be eliminated. Though this is true for the ordinary individual who lacks skillful methods, for the practitioner who possesses skillful means, those very sense objects will help in the attainment of liberation. It is like fire—when out of control, it can cause great damage, but when used properly and skillfully it is very beneficial. While in the lower schools sensory objects are considered as the enemies of religious practice, here they arise as teachers. Moreover, sensory objects are not fetters to realization by their own nature; rather, one is fettered by the erroneous conceptual thoughts that surround them.

The Secret Mantra Vehicle is superior to the Perfection Vehicle from several points of view, but its superiority primarily rests on the greater efficacy and skillfulness of its methods. Through Mantrayāna practice, a person of superior faculties can attain awakening in a single lifetime. One of middling faculties who observes the commitments will attain enlightenment within seven to sixteen lifetimes. These are much shorter periods than the three immeasurable eons required through the Perfection Vehicle practices. But even though the Secret Mantra Vehicle is superior in skillful methods, its view of ultimate reality is identical with the Madhyamaka view of the general Mahāyāna. For both schools, ultimate reality is devoid of all discursive developments or elaborations. One view cannot be higher than the other since higher and lower are themselves but discursive developments or conceptualizations.

The foregoing explanation has provided a general introduction to a few of the basic ideas of Buddhist tantra. The real question is how to apply these theoretical considerations in a useful way—that is, how to practice them. The practice of Mantrayāna and further in-depth study of its philosophy require first of all a special initiation from a qualified master. Before you can be initiated, you will first be examined by the teacher, who will ascertain whether you are a fit receptacle for the teachings. Your master may require that you purify and prepare yourself through specific preparatory practices. Finally, after you have been led into the glorious maṇḍala by the master, you begin your practice, carefully observing the various vows and commitments of the Vajrayāna. These vows are primarily mental, and as such, they can be even more challenging than those of the prātimokṣa and bodhisattva systems. You must also devote yourself to further study and to practicing specialized visualizations and yogas according to the master's instructions.

Buddhist tantra is thus distinguished from the other branches of Mahāyāna by its special methods. It is, however, identical to Mahāyāna Madhyamaka in its ultimate view, and it is the same as all Mahāyāna schools in terms of its aim and motivation. Hindu tantra, by contrast, has a different philosophical basis and motivation, even though it shares some of the same practical methodology. Some persons have suggested that Buddhist tantra must not belong to pure Buddhism because it shares many elements of practice with the Hindus. This is specious reasoning, because certain methods are bound to be shared by different religious traditions. Suppose we had to abandon each and every element of practice shared with Hindu traditions. In that case, we would have to give up generosity, morality, and much more.

There are, of course, many further differences between Buddhist and Hindu tantras in their terminologies, their philosophies, the details of their meditative practices, and so forth. But I shall not attempt to explicate them since my own firsthand knowledge is limited to the Buddhist tradition. Here it will suffice to stress that Buddhist Vajrayāna presupposes the taking of refuge in the Buddha, Dharma, and Saṅgha (and the guru as the embodiment of these three), the understanding of emptiness, and the cultivation of loving-kindness, compassion, and bodhicitta, which is the firm resolve to attain perfect buddhahood in order to benefit all sentient creatures, through the great wish that they be happy and free from sorrow. These distinguishing features are not found in the non-Buddhist tantras.

The study of tantra can only be fruitful if you apply it practice, and to do this you must find, serve, and carefully follow a qualified master. If you find your true teacher and are graced by his or her blessings, you can make swift progress toward the goal—perfect awakening for the benefit of all creatures. In composing this account, I am mindful of my own immeasurable debt of gratitude to my own kind masters. Here I have tried to be true to their teachings and to those of the great masters of our lineage without divulging that which is forbidden to be taught publicly. I shall consider my efforts to be worthwhile if some harmful misunderstandings are dispelled.

Part Four

Dharma in Present Lives, Future Lives, and the World

12. Overcoming Anger and Obstacles

As we have learned, a life focused only on physical happiness or physical comfort is not enough. No matter how good or how luxurious a life you may lead, unless your inner mind is happy, then it is of no real use. One must find real inner peace, peace that endures, and happiness that is permanent.

As a Buddhist, I will describe the Buddhist point of view about how to make our lives more happy and peaceful. We have many different kinds of physical suffering and mental suffering. There are many different methods to treat physical suffering. For example, when you have a disease you can take medicine, or when you have a wound you can apply bandages to it. But mental suffering cannot be cured just by taking medicines, having good facilities, or giving various treatments. The only way to treat mental suffering is to change your way of thinking, the way your mind works, and thus the way you face the vicissitudes of life. This can help a great deal.

Toward this end, I think the Buddha's teachings can help. His Holiness the Dalai Lama advises us of three different categories of Buddhist teaching: Buddhist religion, Buddhist philosophy, and Buddhist science. The Buddhist religion is for Buddhist people only—that is, people who have taken vows, received initiations, and so on. But Buddhist philosophy and Buddhist science are available for anybody to listen to and learn from. Even without becoming a Buddhist, anybody can learn the Buddha's teachings and the Buddha's philosophy, and this can help you to understand the meaning of life and how to face difficulties in your life.

In our everyday life we face many difficulties. Without any kind of spiritual advice to follow, our problems can become severe and unbearable, even when they are only physical pains. But learning certain ways of thinking can change your experience and reduce the degree of your suffering, even though you may not be completely cured of suffering.

One of the Buddha's important teachings is that all compounded things are impermanent. This means that the many different feelings and different kinds of situations we encounter in daily life have not just happened accidentally. None of it just happened without cause. And none of it happened from the wrong cause. Rather, each and every thing has its own cause and its own conditions.

A very good example of this is television. In order for pictures to appear on a television screen, you need many things. You need electricity, you need a machine, you need wires, and you need antennae. When all these conditions are together, then the picture will appear. If any of these things are missing, if even a tiny wire is missing, the picture will not appear. This is nothing other than the operation of causes and conditions. When the appropriate causes and conditions come together, then the phenomenon will appear. If any of the necessary causes and conditions are missing, it will not appear. This means that anything that is dependent on causes and conditions is impermanent. On a television screen, a picture may appear without interruption for a while, but if suddenly the power goes off, the picture will not appear. If suddenly a wire breaks, the picture will not appear. This is impermanence; everything is changing. As long as a phenomenon depends upon causes and conditions, it is defined as impermanent.

The impermanence of all compounded things leads to what we call the four endings. First, the end of gathering is separation. Many people may be gathered together, as we have gathered together today. But at the end of this will be separation. We will not all stay here forever, and everyone will later go to their own place. This ending also applies to our lives as a whole. When we are with family, we can slip into the habit of thinking that the gathering is forever. We did not consciously choose to be born into this particular family. Due to our own deeds, our own karma, we were born into it, and we live gathered together, as father, mother, brother, sister, wife, husband, child, and so on. But no family remains forever. One day, someone will pass away. Another day, someone else will pass away. Father will pass away, then mother will pass away. A spouse will pass away or a child will pass away. You too will pass away. In the end, all will be gone. This is impermanence. There is no such thing as a gathering that never disperses. Thus it is said, "The end of gathering is separation."

Next, the end of accumulation is exhaustion. No matter how much wealth you gain, how many possessions you gather, or how much power you obtain, none of it will remain. After a while, it will all be exhausted and will be lost. History records many great empires that owned nearly the entire world, and not one of these empires remains. They have all disintegrated. Even great empires eventually lose territory and become small. All will be finished.

Additionally, the end of rising high is falling. No matter what height you reach, you must eventually come back down. In ancient times there were said to be universal emperors who ruled many continents. But they did not remain rulers for all time. Similarly, no matter what high position you attain, you will not remain there forever. After a while, something will happen, and you will fall. Therefore, the end of rising high is to fall down.

Finally, the end of birth is death. Anyone who is born in this world has to die. There is no one who is born who will not die. There is not even the slightest doubt about this. There have been many great historical figures, many great spiritual practitioners, many great statesmen, and many great heroes. Today they are just history. They did not remain.

All compounded things are like this. Therefore, the Buddha taught impermanence. One of the most common wrong views is the perception that life is permanent. Of course, if life were permanent, then it would be true that we need wealth and power. But if life is impermanent, then what is the use of having so much wealth, what is the use of having so much power, when sooner or later you are going to lose it? And when this happens, you are going to face even greater suffering. It is better not to have strong attachments. Attachment is one of the main causes of suffering. When you have strong attachment, you become angry at other people who have power, who have prosperity, who have wealth. Anger can lead to other negative emotions as well, such as jealousy. And when you have anger, jealousy, and attachment, you will never experience peace.

Thus we see that the mental suffering and anxieties encountered in everyday life are not caused by outside factors. They are caused by your own negative emotions. The minute anger arises in your mind you no longer experience peace. Anger not only disturbs your own peace of mind, it disturbs your immediate circle, your family members, your neighborhood, and, in a larger sense, the whole world. Indeed, the greatest problems we face in today's world arise from anger.

Even if we realize that anger is a primary cause of suffering, it is difficult to control it straight away. But if we know that anger is the cause of our suffering, then at least we can feel some motivation to change and we can do something to calm down. The minute you calm your anger, you can experience peace in your mind. And then you can experience peace within your family, within your neighborhood, and in the whole world.

We should not cast blame externally for the problems that we face, but instead we should try to see how the problems arise internally. A person who does not have anger cannot have enemies. The person who has anger naturally has many enemies. Enemies are a reflection of your own anger, in the same way that your face is reflected in a mirror. When you have anger, this inner anger is reflected back and the enemy appears outside. If you try to destroy your enemy with anger, the other side will also become angry, and the situation will escalate. Even if you destroy one enemy, there will be another enemy, and more and more enemies will arise. Instead of defeating outside enemies, you should look toward your own anger as the real enemy, the enemy that causes suffering. The real enemy is not outside but within your own mind. Even if you cannot eliminate your anger entirely, trying to see things this way will help you to disrupt it.

It is very difficult to totally conquer anger because we have been associated with it for such a long period of time, and we have formed habitual tendencies that have built up and cause it to recur. We know, for example, that certain behaviors such as drinking and smoking are harmful. Everyone knows that smoking is harmful, but a person who is used to it has formed a habit that is hard to break. Even though every package states very clearly that smoking is injurious to one's health, those who are already in the habit of smoking cannot give it up. Likewise, we know that anger is harmful, even in this life. When you have anger, then you cannot experience peace and happiness. You also lose your appetite, lose sleep, lose comfort in your daily life. It is unmistakably harmful.

Further, when your mind is disturbed, many physical diseases also arise. When your mind is very unhappy, and you experience great tension or anxiety, this causes diseases like high blood pressure. Many doctors have told me this. Anger is plainly very harmful, and if something is harmful then we should not do it.

Even trying to think about this will help. Instead of directing anger outwardly, see that the problems, difficulties, and negative circumstances that we face in everyday life do not come from the outside but come mainly from our own negative emotions like anger.

Why, then, do we have anger in the first place? The answer is that anger and attachment are like two sides of the same coin. When you have strong attachment, then anger arises. This understanding arises from the basic Buddhist view that there are three main negative emotions. First, all negative emotions derive from ignorance, which means not knowing the true nature of reality. Instead of seeing the truth, we are in ignorance and do not understand. From ignorance arise anger and desire. When you have these three—anger, desire, and ignorance—then pride, jealousy, and many other negative emotions arise. When you have negative emotions, you take actions— physical, verbal, and mental—that create patterns that dominate your whole life, and the result is that we all suffer. Our negative emotions constantly make us suffer physically and mentally. Therefore, instead of blaming others we have to look at our own negative emotions. The enemy is not outside. The enemy is within our own mind. Our own negative emotions are the cause of the difficulties and problems we face.

As I have explained, the Buddha taught that everything is impermanent. This perception of impermanence is very important. Usually we think that life is permanent. We make plans for our lives with the idea that we will be here forever, and so we think that we must acquire possessions, we must have power, we must have this, we must have that. This is attachment. Then, when we lose these things, we become angry. Therefore, the main problem is attachment. But if you think of impermanence, you see that you are going to lose everything one day. Even if you have an entire kingdom, you are going to lose it, so why have strong attachment? Why hold on so tightly when sooner or later you are assuredly going to lose what you have? This thought helps very much in relieving tension and anxiety.

Buddhists understand there to be two different kinds of impermanence. The first is what we call "gradual" or "gross" impermanence. This means that everything is changing. For example, our physical body is changing. The baby becomes a child, the child becomes a teenager, the teenager becomes an adult. An adult becomes middle-aged, and the middle-aged become old. As you become old, your body changes further. The color of your hair, the texture of your skin, your face—everything changes. This impermanence or constant change in the things we see is called "gross continual impermanence." Outwardly, we can also see that places are changing. In the summertime we have one color, then in autumn we have the beautiful colors of the autumn leaves, then comes the white of winter, which is very different. Then come the bright colors of spring, and so on. Everything is changing.

By examining gross impermanence, we can gain an understanding of subtle impermanence. Changes we see do not occur overnight. For example, consider the color of our hair. If yesterday it was black, today it will not suddenly change to white. The change is acquired subtly all the time. Therefore, it is called "subtle momentary change." This means that change is actually happening constantly, at every single moment, all the way down to the very shortest possible interval of time. Therefore, when you see the colors of the season change, or your skin color or hair color change, you can understand these changes as subtle, infinitesimal changes that build up to a larger, more visible change. The major visible changes imply a subtle process of constant, invisible change.

The Buddha's teaching on impermanence is a great help. Contemplating impermanence, you know that you are going to lose your possessions, that your hair color is going to change, and that your body is going to change. You know that you will not be here forever; everything is subject to change. Such recollections naturally reduce the degree of attachment. As attachment lessens, anger also naturally lessens. There is no point in fighting and quarreling when sooner or later we are all going to lose. Sooner or later, all of us are going to change. Sooner or later, all of us are going to die. Therefore, what is the point?

While we are here today as living beings, we should live to make everyone happy, everyone peaceful, and everyone prosperous. And in order to do this, we have to feel other people's feelings. When you think about yourself alone, when you care only for your own well-being, your own happiness, your own suffering, or your own things, then you can never achieve real peace.

Just as you yourself wish to be free from suffering and long for happiness, so too does every human being—in fact, every living being. Instead of thinking of yourself alone, it is crucial to think of others. It is helpful to think of yourself not as all-important but as an example of the situation of all beings. In your own life, you wish to be healthy and happy. All beings have the same wish. When we compare ourselves to others, others are actually more important. After all, you are just one person. But when you think of others, there are countless others. Countless others are certainly more important than just one, so you must think of others, their well-being, their happiness, their suffering.

Thinking carefully about impermanence and suffering helps to lessen our own difficulties, our own problems, our own sufferings. On this basis, we can gradually move toward the ultimate aim of achieving everlasting peace and happiness. But to accomplish this, I always advise patience. Everyone wants the best of everything. Even in the spiritual path, everyone wishes to follow the highest path, the most advanced path, the deepest path, the most profound path. Of course, in worldly life, you want the best food, the best house, the best life. But when it comes to actually practicing the highest spiritual path, are you really ready? If not, it will not work. If you want to ride the best and the most powerful horse, you need strength. If you do not have the requisite strength but you still attempt to ride the best and most powerful horse, you will experience problems. Along similar lines, I always advise that, whether you are Buddhist or non-Buddhist, whatever philosophy you follow, it is better at first to concentrate on becoming a good human being. Indeed, if you are not a good human being, how can you become a good spiritual practitioner?

In ancient times society was divided into different classes like the priestly class, the royal class, the general class, the lower class, and so on. The Buddha was actually the first revolutionary, the first to declare people from all classes equal. The Buddha said that there is no such thing as being born higher class or lower class. He said that everyone is equal. A person who is truthful and honest and lives a virtuous life—such a person is of the highest class. Thus it is not the family into which one is born but what one does that places a person in the highest class.

It is very important to feel this way. The Buddha said that everyone is equal because, according to the Buddhist teachings, everyone has buddha nature. This means that by meeting with the right method, by meeting with the right path, anyone can become a buddha. Everyone has this opportunity. This is true not only of human beings but of animals. Every living being has buddha nature, and therefore every living being can become a buddha. This is, of course, our main goal. Because everyone has buddha nature, if we implement the right methods, then we can all become buddhas. But to reach that level, first we have to be good human beings. A good human being is one who does not dwell on selfish thoughts. Selfish people cannot experience peace, cannot experience happiness, and cannot be good human beings. A good human being is someone who is truthful, honest, and who cares for others.

Just as you yourself wish to achieve happiness, every living being also has the same goal. Instead of thinking of your own well-being, think of others. It will help you to face everyday difficulties. Thus, when we enter the spiritual path, first it is very important to learn to be a good human being. On the basis of becoming a good human being, then we can follow the spiritual path. Follow whichever path is suitable for you, and by following that path, you can achieve your spiritual goal.

13. Stages of the Bardo

DEATH RESULTS FROM the exhaustion of these three things: life, merit, and karma. If only one of these factors is exhausted, it is possible to revive quite easily, and death can then be prevented by doing certain practices. For example, if life is exhausted, then by doing long-life deity practices your life will be replenished, and you can continue living for some time. If karma is exhausted, then by performing positive actions or karma, it is possible to replenish the karma of living. If two of the factors are exhausted, then it will be more difficult to prevent death. When all three are exhausted, death is inescapable, and one has to leave this world.

Bardo means the intermediate state, the time in between the end of the present life and the beginning of the next life. Most people will go through the bardo after they die, but it is said that there are two types of persons who will not enter the bardo. First, there are those who are very advanced in practice, so that right after exiting the body, the consciousness immediately enters a buddha field or pure realm. Second, there are those who have very heavy negative karma. Right after dying, these people will go directly to the lower realms. Generally speaking, there are three lower realms: the hell realm, the hungry ghost realm, and the animal realm. However, this type of person goes directly to the lowest, the hell realm.

For the majority of people, when consciousness leaves the body, it will enter the bardo. Advanced teachings describe different lights that are seen at the time of death. Those who will be born in the god realm perceive a white light. Those who will be born in the hungry ghost realm perceive a yellow light; in the animal realm, a blue light; in the demigod realm, a red light; and in the hell realm, a black light. Those who will be born in the human realm perceive a multicolored or green light, because green is said to be a combination of many different colors.

In the bardo, there is just a mental body without the physical body. In this state, beings have a very difficult time, because there is so much disarray. Consciousness is like a feather blown every which way by the wind. The feather is very light and is blown wherever the wind takes it. Likewise the bardo consciousness travels very fast, in the same way that the mind can move very fast. It can travel anywhere, to any part of the universe, instantaneously. When you are in motion like this, however, there is no consistency, only a turbulent series of indefinite experiences and encounters with different companions, different places, different foods, and different lifestyles. These are all changing all of the time, and the situation produces great anxiety. So there are no patterns, no companions, and no friends in the bardo; it is constantly changing.

Many people do not even know that they have died. They will try to speak to their relatives and friends, but no one will respond to them. Living people, of course, cannot see bardo beings or hear their voices. However, beings in the bardo, unlike in our present state, possess a kind of intuition or a contaminated wisdom, so they are aware not only of what other people are doing but also of what they are thinking. I believe that this is because, lacking a physical body and dwelling only in a very subtle mental state, they are able see other people's minds and can know what they are thinking. Seeing other people's jealousy and pride and anger and so forth causes bardo beings to become very agitated. It affects them if other people neglect them, ignore them, do not take care of them, or think badly about them.

Also, they can see the things that belonged to them be taken away by various people, and they accumulate a lot of defilements like desire, hatred, jealousy, pride, and so forth. Bardo beings accumulate a lot of defilements. Therefore, after death, during the forty-nine days of rituals we perform in our tradition, it is very important to explain to the deceased that they are no longer living. It is important to make sure that they realize that they are deceased and, at the moment, in the bardo.

The mental body of a bardo being has its own faculties for sensory perceptions—its own eyes, ears, nose, tongue, and so forth. Because this body is mental and not physical, it can go through mountains and walls, as well as to any place in the universe. It cannot, however, pass through very holy places, like the stupa in Bodh Gaya, for example. It also cannot pass through the womb of a mother that it does not have the karma to enter. Otherwise, it can travel anywhere.

Bardo beings, lacking physical bodies, cannot take in any substantial food. They can only find some satisfaction by taking in the scent of food. Depending upon the strength of the being, they will chase after the scent of food. Those who have more strength are able to take in smells. That is the reason why we make burnt offerings for them during the forty-nine days after death.

The above general description of the bardo is known to all of the different yānas, or vehicles of Buddhism.

I will now describe aspects of the bardo that are special to Mahāyāna teachings. These teachings describe seven fearful conditions, which include four fearful sounds and three fearful chasms or cliffs.

The first of the four fearful sounds is the sound of a mountain splitting apart or cracking. Our body is created from the four elements, and it is maintained with the four elements, and its exhaustion is the exhaustion of the four elements. The first fearful sound occurs when the element of earth is absorbed into the element of water, and there manifests a sound like that of mountain cracking apart.

When the element of water is absorbed into the element of fire, there is a sound like the shaking of all of the oceans. When the element of fire is absorbed into the element of air, there is a sound like that of the great fire at the end of an eon. And when the element of air is absorbed into the element of consciousness, there is the sound of the great storm at the end of an eon.

Then the experiences of the three fearful cliffs arise. These cliffs are like falling into the three lower realms—the hell realm, the hungry ghost realm, and the animal realm. Hearing these four fearful sounds and seeing these very frightening cliffs produces a fearful state and great anxiety. You will be inclined to seek refuge wherever you can. At that time, it is very important to remember the Triple Gem—the Buddha, Dharma, and Saṅgha.

The bardo has six uncertainties. The first one is the uncertainty of place. There is no permanent place in the bardo because beings in the bardo have no physical body, only a mental body. The mental body can travel very far in the bardo—sometimes to very nice places like celestial palaces, but sometimes also to hell realms, and so on.

The second uncertainty is the uncertainty of companions. This means there are no permanent companions or friends. Friends, enemies, or indifferent, unknown beings of all kinds may accompany you at any given moment in the bardo.

The third is the uncertainty of food. Sometimes food is like nectar, but sometimes food consists of very dirty things. It is constantly changing. Beings in the bardo have only a mental body, and the mental substitute for the sense organs cannot enjoy solid food. In the bardo the senses can be satisfied only by the smell of burning food.

The fourth uncertainty is the uncertainty of refuge. The bardo has four terrifying sounds and three very dangerous cliffs. There is much anxiety and fear as one desperately seeks refuge in all kinds of places from all kinds of beings.

The fifth uncertainty is the uncertainty of mental state, which changes constantly. All kinds of thoughts can rise.

The sixth and final uncertainty is the uncertainty of feelings. All kinds of feelings arise in the bardo; happy feelings, unhappy feelings, and even indifferent feelings. Even in a single moment different kinds of feelings can arise.

Also, according to the higher teachings, everything that exists, the whole of the outside world that we experience, arises as if from seeds within our body. For example, because bardo beings have no white or red element in their bodies, they see no sun or moon. It is because of the inner red and white elements that the sun and moon are perceived.

There is no definite rule, but average people remain in the bardo state for seven weeks. This is why we do memorial practices for forty-nine days. During the first half of the bardo period, bardo beings have strong feelings or inclinations toward their previous life, the life that they just departed. During the second half, they will have stronger visions and more inclinations regarding their future life. Also, each week, they experience another death. Of course, this is not real death as such, but they experience a kind of death and once again assume a mental body.

Usually, forty-nine days after dying, most people take rebirth into one of the six realms. But this is not necessarily the case. It is said that even after many eons some people cannot take rebirth and they still roam around in the bardo.

Because beings in the bardo state are very anxious and fearful, it is difficult to remember the guru and the Triple Gem. But if one can remember them, because there are no physical limitations in the bardo as it is only a mental state, then it will be very easy to achieve realization.

14. Dharma in Everyday Life

THE MOST IMPORTANT thing is spiritual practice. All other things, such as material wealth or power, are only beneficial within this lifespan. On the day we leave this world, we will have to leave everything behind—our wealth, our friends, even our precious body. Only consciousness will be left, and when this happens, the only thing that we can rely upon will be our spiritual practice.

Even when we face major problems in this life, there is a vast difference between the person who has spiritual assistance and the one who does not. When the person without any spiritual assistance faces such suffering, they are in a desperate situation and have to rely on wrong methods, perhaps taking extreme measures. One of the basic teachings of the Buddha is that everything created by causes and conditions is impermanent. Additionally, any actions connected with defilements cause suffering. Therefore, when we face problems, it is clear that they are not anomalies that happen just to us. Rather, impermanence and suffering are the nature of existence itself. Someone who understands this is more prepared to face problems. The problem itself, externally, might remain unchanged, but the suffering is reduced. A person who has spiritual assistance is better prepared to face a problem because he knows its true nature. This understanding lessens the mental burden, and when your mental burden is lessened, outer physical suffering diminishes. The mind is the boss and the body is like a servant. If the mind is happy, you could be in even the poorest conditions but still be happy. And if the mind is not happy, even if you have the best facilities, you will feel a lot of misery. Since the mind is the most important factor that gives us strength to face the challenges of suffering even in this life, the most important thing we can do is practice Dharma.

Śāntideva said, "All sufferings in this universe come from caring for oneself." If we think of ourselves, we have jealousy, pride, stinginess, desire, hatred, and so forth. All manner of impure thoughts arise, and any actions created with these impure thoughts create only suffering. Śāntideva also said, "All happiness in this universe comes from wanting others to be happy." If we wish others to be happy, then all good things and all good qualities come. Similarly, on the basis of loving-kindness and compassion, if we want to help other sentient beings, any actions that we create produce happiness. That is why the root of the Mahāyāna teachings is loving-kindness and compassion. Therefore, we must try in every way to cultivate loving-kindness and compassion.

However, merely having compassion is not enough. We must rescue sentient beings from suffering and put them on the path of happiness. But at the moment we ourselves are not free. We do not have full knowledge or full power. We are completely bound by our own karma and defilements. So how can we help? The sole most effective way to help sentient beings is to attain perfect enlightenment, because if we attain perfect enlightenment then even during a single moment we can rescue countless sentient beings.

This perfect enlightenment does not arise without proper causes and conditions, and they come from following the Mahāyāna path. The first step is to have a very sincere wish to attain perfect enlightenment. Then you must practice. The main goal of practice is to develop both method and wisdom. In order to fly, you need two wings, and, similarly, in order to attain enlightenment, you need two supports: the method to realize wisdom and wisdom itself. These two depend on each other. Method means the accumulation of merit through generosity, moral conduct, patience, zeal, and concentration. Loving-kindness and compassion will only suppress faults, the chief of which is self-clinging. These methods only suppress self-clinging. In order to completely dig out the root of self-clinging, we require wisdom, which completely eliminates it. To develop wisdom, we must have concentration. With these two together, we will be able to attain perfect enlightenment.

Many people say it is very difficult to practice Dharma, particularly in big cities where there is so much distraction and business to attend to.

However, the Lord Buddha gave many teachings to help us tame our wild minds. Because our mind has been so thoroughly involved with defilements, we have been caught in the realm of existence and so we suffer. We have already suffered so much in the past, and we are still suffering. Furthermore, if we do not start diligently practicing the Dharma now, we will continue to experience suffering ceaselessly. Therefore, the Buddha gave teachings involving many different forms of practice, but all of them serve to tame our mind.

The Sanskrit word *dharma* has many different meanings, but the word generally means to change: to change our impure or wild mind that is so involved with defilements toward the right path. Although of course even just doing practice has some benefit, the point of practice is to change one's mind. If one's mind does not change, then it is not very effective. We must look to see whether the practices we are doing are making a real difference in our mind or not. If the practice changes our mind, then, if we use it in the right way, we could be the busiest person in the busiest city but still be a very good Dharma practitioner because everything we see and do, everyone we associate with, gives us a chance to practice Dharma.

For example, when traveling in cities and noticing many changes, we witness the truth of impermanence. When we see so much suffering, we are experiencing the Buddha's teaching that everything is suffering. The fact that we actually see it with our own naked eyes means we can immediately learn it. When we associate with the vast numbers of people in cities, we have a chance to help them, to practice compassion. When people disturb us or are angry with us, it gives us a chance to practice patience. In this way, if we can apply the teachings to our everyday life, then wherever we are, at work or at home, we can use our experiences and surroundings to practice the Dharma.

These different experiences can help us to understand more deeply how important it is to practice the Dharma. Higher meditations like concentration and insight are very important, but in order to reach that level, it is necessary to cultivate the basic foundations—such as contemplating the difficulty of obtaining precious human birth, impermanence and death, the cause of karma, and the suffering of saṃsāra, together known as the four common foundations. These you can learn from a teacher or study in books.

However, just gaining knowledge is not enough. If we have held the relevant knowledge for a long time, but it has not worked a change within us, then we will remain the same person. We will have the same anger, and we will be unable to proceed in the Dharma. Although we might have heard about the difficulties of obtaining a precious human birth a hundred times, if it has not made a change in us, if we remain on the same level with the same defilements, then this means that we are not really practicing. Why is this so? Because we are not really experiencing the Dharma.

Thus we see that knowing about the Dharma and experiencing it through contemplation are two very different things. You may know many teachings, but if you do not practice them, if you do not use them in your daily life, then this is not right. For example, the purpose of making delicious food is to eat it. If you make it but you do not eat it, there is no point. Similarly, knowing the Dharma only matters when we utilize it in our daily life. To do this, we have to use many different methods, including our daily experiences.

With these basic foundations, if we understand everything we see not only as a teaching but as a spur toward an inner feeling, a spiritual urge, then we will not be wasting our time. We will definitely make every effort, just as people in prison constantly have only one thought, "When can I get out of this place?" When you have this real, sincere desire to practice the Dharma, then your inner, higher meditations will generally arise.

First, having the basic foundations depends on our merit. Due to having accumulated merit in past lives, we have been born as human beings in this life, we have had the good fortune to hear the Dharma, and we have had a chance to practice it. Similarly, having a real inner feeling about spiritual practice depends on the merit that we have accumulated. So we must accumulate merit through prayers, through devotion to the guru and to the Buddha, Dharma, and Saṅgha, and through practicing loving-kindness and compassion toward all sentient beings. In this way, as our merit increases, our wisdom also increases, and these two grow together. When merit is built up, wisdom will also come, and with merit and wisdom together we will be able to succeed on the path.

15. Global Ecology from a Buddhist Perspective

THE LIFE WE HAVE is very precious. We can see this from the way we worry. We worry about falling sick, we worry that somebody may attack us, and we make every effort to preserve our lives. Nothing is more precious to us than our own lives—not from a religious point of view, but simply from a worldly point of view.

Similarly, every living being also thinks his or her own life is very precious. We do not want to lose this life. We wish to sustain it and continue it for as long as possible. Therefore, it is very important to understand that our lives and the larger environment are connected to each other.

Many of you are already familiar with what we call the "wheel of life." A wheel turns once, turns again, and goes on and on without beginning or end. Similarly, life has no beginning or end as such, and it goes on and on. We have taken birth from beginningless time until now innumerable times, and in the future we will continue to take birth again and again unless we attain liberation or enlightenment. Wherever our defilements and the winds of karma blow, there we must be born. We have no choice. Therefore, there is not a single place where you have not been born.

Furthermore, there is not a single sentient being who has not been our parent, our friend, our partner, our child, and so on. But due to the change of life, we do not recognize each other. We see some people as our friends, some as our enemies, and some as indifferent to us. But in reality, every sentient being is one of our very dear ones.

I think it is important for everybody to realize that because life is precious to oneself, therefore it is also precious to others. When you think about your own feelings, you can learn how every individual also has the same kind of feelings. Not only is life precious for you; it is also precious to every living being, from the tiniest insect to the mightiest god. Therefore, we should remember that life is precious to all beings and concern ourselves with how to protect life.

If life is precious, then we must protect where we live. We cannot live in places with no water, no trees, and so on. All environmental problems, therefore, are connected with our lives. In fact, one can say that the Lord Buddha was the founder of environmentalism because his vinaya contains rules that monastics cannot cut down trees, pluck flowers, disturb the forest, pollute the river, or soil the grass. These are exactly the type of environmental protections we talk about today. A long time ago, the Buddha already laid down these rules for Buddhist monks and nuns.

Also, the Buddha's teachings, especially the Mahāyāna teachings, state that every living being was once our parent, so we must repay the kindness and benefits we received from them. Even our enemies who are harming us were also our very dear ones, but because we do not recognize them, instead of paying them back with kindness, we pay them back with anger. In the Buddha's teachings, love and compassion are described as infinite. There is no exception. We should love everybody, known and unknown, near and far, loved and hated. Everybody should have equal love and compassion toward every sentient being.

The present world faces many environmental problems. Many people fear that in a matter of years, the world will be a desert. There will be no water, no trees, no rain, and so much pollution in the air that everybody will have to carry around oxygen tanks to breathe! Therefore, it is very important to think about our planet for the sake of our future generations. The Buddha's teachings are deep and wide; everything is included. But Buddhists mainly devote their time and energy to practices such as meditation, so they do not conduct many external activities. By contrast, environmentalists are very active; they do many things to directly help animals and plants and so on. The difference between modern environmentalists and Buddhists is that the former are more practical, whereas the latter take a deeper and wider view.

Modern environmentalists consider life as precious, and they do not just talk, but they actively work to protect life. However, their approach is incomplete. For example, in India, many people are worried about protecting tigers. It is said that India used to have forty thousand tigers, but now the number has drastically dropped to only fourteen thousand tigers. Tigers are very beautiful and powerful and nice, so environmentalists wish to protect them. They also focus on animals that need to be protected because they are rare, such as some species of deer in India. Anyone who hunts those deer faces severe punishments. This is very good.

But we do not only need to protect rare and beautiful animals; life is for everybody. And yet, there are no environmentalists who say that we need to protect mosquitoes. Perhaps they don't want to protect them because mosquitoes are very ugly and noisy, and they disturb and bite you, and they carry diseases such as malaria. Therefore, even environmentalists think it is better to destroy mosquitoes. But mosquitoes are also living beings. All life is precious.

Buddhist teachings tell us that every living being needs to be protected, whether they are harmful or beneficial to us, whether they are beautiful or ugly, plentiful or rare. In India, you are allowed to shoot some wild animals that are plentiful. From the Buddhist point of view, this is not correct. Practically, not everybody will agree on this. But from a Buddhist perspective, the main point is that life is precious, to ourselves and also to mosquitoes. Indeed, mosquitoes' lives are very short; some of them live for only a day or two. But even though they do not have much time to live, whenever people see mosquitoes, unfortunately, they kill them.

The Buddhist idea of protecting life with love and compassion is much deeper and wider than a single species. Yet not all Buddhists carry this into practice. Some Buddhists may meditate and recite prayers saying, "May all sentient beings be happy and have the cause of happiness," yet when animals nearby are suffering or crying, they are not bothered.

On the other hand, environmentalists and other humanitarians may not say prayers or meditate, but they go into the field where animals are suffering, crying, and sick, and help them. I think this is very good.

Therefore, I think we should combine these two together: the Buddha's teachings of universal compassion and compassionate people's active environmental work. If we combine these two, I think it would be of great benefit. It will be much more powerful and much wider than either approach alone.

Right from the beginning, the Buddha himself taught that life is precious, so therefore we should make this world beautiful and clean, not only for human beings, but for the sake of animals, too—in fact, for all sentient beings.

There is a story of a monk who was meditating, and suddenly a banana leaf fell on him and disturbed him. He got very angry and crushed the leaf and said, "Why did the Buddha make such a strange rule of not allowing monks to pluck leaves and flowers?" and he felt anger toward the Buddha.

So in his next life, he was born as a nāga with a huge tree growing on his head. The growing tree was very painful and heavy as the root was growing downward, and so the former monk suffered greatly. At one point, when the Buddha was traveling with a king, he came across the monk. The king asked the Buddha, "Why does this nāga have a tree on his head and suffer so?" The Buddha replied that in a previous life, this person was a monk who grew angry, crushed a banana leaf, and disrespected the rules that the Buddha had laid down. As a consequence, he was born into his current life.

This story shows how much the Buddha was concerned about trees, flowers, water, streams, pools, and so on. I think it is important for modern environmentalists to take ideas from the Buddha's teachings, especially the rules of the vinaya.

Of course we cannot protect everything and everyone, but we should do whatever we can. Environmental protection is not something that only one individual or organization can do. It is something that everybody must do; everybody has this responsibility. First of all, it is very important to make people aware of the dangers that will arise in the future if we do not take care of the environment. In many ways it is already too late; we cannot protect the environment for everybody everywhere. But if we are aware and many individuals make an effort, we will certainly produce a definite and concrete result.

The main thing everyone should realize is that life is precious. If life is precious, then we must do something. We must protect this world because many things are already changing. For example, many of my friends in Tibet have told me that the climate in Tibet is changing. The snow is melting, and the rate of melting is increasing. Consequently, the water and climate are changing and growing disturbed.

We believe these changes affect not only that which is visible, such as mountains, trees, and so on, but also that which is invisible. In Tibet, every mountain has its own local deities that reside there. Ancient beliefs say that they can also be disturbed. If they are not happy or healthy, it will create disaster in the outside world.

I think this phenomenon is due to people becoming too greedy. They cut too many trees, doing all kinds of mining and so on, disturbing the trees, mountains, ground, water, and everything. These disturbances also affect the spirits and deities. Many people do not believe in local deities and the like. But I think there is definitely something going on. Due to all these changes, we face many disasters like earthquakes, tsunamis, fires, and tornadoes; all kinds of problems arise. I believe these phenomena are all connected to one another.

So not only do we have to protect the environment, but we must also rejuvenate mother earth herself. For that, we must do rituals. There are many rituals that could help, such as burying treasure vases, bathing rituals, incense offerings, and so on. Doing these things will certainly have a very good effect. For example, Taiwan and Japan have earthquakes quite often, sometimes very severe ones. But lately, many Taiwanese Buddhist masters have performed offering rituals, fire rituals, bathing rituals, and treasure vase burials. Many people have told me that since then, there are fewer earthquakes and typhoons. Not everybody believes this, but I think that by trying methods from every angle and every tradition, conditions will definitely improve.

Again, protecting the environment is not something only a few individuals or a few organizations can accomplish. Everyone has responsibility because we are all human beings, and we have to think about future generations of human beings. For the sake of future generations' well-being, we must act now. Otherwise, our future generations will have to live as though they are in a land of hungry ghosts. This would be a tragic outcome. Therefore, while we are alive, we should make efforts to protect the environment. First, it is important to feel in the depth of our hearts how precious life is and how important it is to make this life healthier, happier, longer, and more sustainable.

In this way, I think it is very important to adopt the teachings of the Buddha, who possesses omniscient wisdom. The Buddha's wisdom is infinite. He sees all of the past, present, and future just like we see our own palms, very clearly, knowing each and every cause and effect. Therefore, the teachings he gave are great, wondrous, and most authentic. The teachings of the Buddha encourage us to work for the benefit of the world and the environment. This will be of great benefit. Therefore, I sincerely hope everyone will make some effort to preserve and sustain the environment.

16. Advice from a Spiritual Friend

You speak from your own culture and heritage. You speak so confidently about the loving-kindness of our mothers, our family, and our friends. But in this culture there are so many who come from dysfunctional, disharmonious, and unloving family relationships. This makes it very difficult for us to hear you mention loving and nurturing people, especially in the family. Can you comment on this?

The teachings are given to people to eliminate suffering and obtain liberation. It is true that it is difficult to practice loving-kindness and compassion, especially in this age. The pith instructions and teachings have been passed down from one guru to the next for many generations. Receiving them, even if you cannot practice all of them, can be very helpful. The Buddha's teachings are like the ocean, very deep and wide. Whatever you can take from them, even a single spoonful, will be of great benefit. Moreover, we all need loving-kindness; it is basic to our human nature. Therefore, we must try to cultivate it through following the teachings and carrying our efforts into every aspect of our lives.

How can we effectively eliminate or deal with fear in our daily life?

The great Indian master Śāntideva said, "If what we fear is something we can change, then there is no need to worry about or fear it. But if it is something beyond our control that we cannot change, then there is no point in worrying about or fearing it."

How can we counteract the pride that arises in a situation where you know you are doing a good job or are good in a particular area?

As it is said, "On the basis of pride, no good qualities remain." So if you wish to have good qualities, you must eliminate pride by contemplating examples of great beings who humbly serve and effectively help other beings.

Can a buddha see the impure vision in addition to the pure vision?

There are different explanations. But according to our tradition, a buddha does not see the impure vision. As I mentioned before, a buddha is like a man who has awakened from sleep and therefore does not see his dreams.

Your Holiness, could you please say a little about the ngakpa *tradition of the Sakya school?*

Ngakpa actually means *mantradara*, or "mantra practitioner." All Tibetan Buddhists are mantradaras; all Tibetan Buddhists are ngakpas. But in the Tibetan social system, ngakpa lay practitioners are mostly hereditary lineage holders such as myself; lay practitioners from a hereditary lineage are called "mantradaras" or "ngakpas."

Your Holiness, how do we go about finding a teacher to guide us through all these points that you talked about today, and how can we know who our guru is?

Finding a spiritual master is very important, for the source of all good qualities is the spiritual master. Spiritual masters should have many qualifications. But the minimum qualification should be someone who has compassion, knowledge, and wisdom: the compassion to teach disciples, the knowledge of what to teach, and the wisdom to see the nature of reality.

Are there factors that determine at what time during this or future lifetimes the fruit of a person's virtuous actions will manifest? What are the factors?

It depends on the action itself. There are certain actions whose fruit will ripen in this life. When the object toward whom it is practiced is strong, the action is strong, and the intention is strong, then the result ripens in this very lifetime. Certain actions ripen in this life, after this lifetime, or even several lifetimes later. The law of cause and effect is such a subtle thing that no ordinary person can fully explain it.

Sakya Paṇḍita was very critical of the use of the term mahāmudrā *in connection with the highest completion practices. Would you comment on this in connection with the other schools of Tibetan Buddhism?*

In fact, Sakya Paṇḍita did not say that we could not use the term *mahāmudrā*. As with any practice, not just mahāmudrā, if we do not do it correctly, we cannot achieve the result. If we do it correctly, with the right teacher, the right path, and the right method, we can achieve the result. What he said was that in order to attain enlightenment, we must follow the right practices that balance method and wisdom. Mahāmudrā is the primordial wisdom that we experience through meditation.

Please explain the concept of karma and its relationship to cause and effect and merit.

The word *karma* actually means "action" or "activities"—the work that we undertake. Our lives and all of the experiences we go through now are the product of our own past actions. No one else can make us suffer. No one else can make us happy. Only through the main cause, which is our own actions, will we be happy or suffer. The actions that we have taken create the effect and the result.

What is the difference between ultimate reality, or emptiness, and nothingness? And where does spontaneous primordial wisdom come from?

Nothingness and ultimate reality are vastly different. Nothingness is void. Ordinary people see everything as existing and consider this life as existing. But if you say it does not exist at all, then that is the opposite extreme. Ultimate reality is away from both existing and nonexisting. On the relative level, there are logical extremes of existing, nonexisting, both, or neither. But ultimate reality is beyond our present relative perception, beyond any description of this and that. We can experience this, but we cannot express it in words.

How do you reconcile the Buddha's teachings that everyone should question what they hear and validate each point themselves with the emphasis on the importance of faith?

The Buddha himself said that you should examine the teachings that he gave, just as you would examine gold you consider buying to make sure it is genuine. Only when you are convinced it is genuine gold will you buy it. Similarly, the teachings of the Buddha should not be accepted through faith, but through reason. The faith created through reason is of course much more authentic. So you should examine the Buddha's teachings in relation to your own life.

Can a person born without the conditions for spiritual development decide to seek the path and create the spiritual conditions for spiritual development?

The general Mahāyāna teachings describe requirements that entail certain conditions. But in the higher Vajrayāna, even those who lack the general conditions can proceed. Since every sentient being possesses buddha nature, every sentient being has the potential to develop full enlightenment. Therefore, even those who lack the right conditions, with the help of spiritual masters, can at least enroll in the path.

Let us consider a person who lives in an area where there is war and consequently suffers from the war. Is it due to their karma that they were born in an area where there is war? For example, how do you explain the karma of those who suffered in World War II?

Yes. The Buddha's teachings state that all lives that we go through are due to our karma. There is both individual karma and collective karma. Karma has three types of results. The first type of result is, for example, if you do a negative deed, you fall down into a lower realm and experience great suffering. The second type of result is that even if you are free from the lower realms, you still suffer. This is called "result similar to the cause." For example, by killing animals or by shortening an animal's life, you will also experience short life and sickness. The third kind of result has to do with habits. In the past, if you performed repetitive negative deeds, they become a habit. For example, if in a past life people repeatedly took life, in this life they enjoy hunting.

Is the buddhahood of a deity different from the buddhas?

As I mentioned before, deities are actually the ultimate Buddha or primordial wisdom taking different forms in order to help beings. For example, there are peaceful deities and wrathful deities. And there are some very simple deities and some very elaborate deities, depending on the level of the practitioner's mind. There are deities to suit every level. The deities also have very special symbolic meanings.

If you concentrate on an image, what size should it be?

There is no specific size, but it should be something you can easily encompass within your field of vision. If something is very huge, then you cannot see it as a whole. So it is good to use a size that is adequate for your eyes to see.

How do we practice compassion every day in an urban setting? What do we do for the homeless and beggars on the train?

We must have compassion that is within our limits. We cannot do everything. We cannot help everybody. Some things are not within our power, but as much as our individual power allows, we should try to help.

Your Holiness, what is your view of freedom for spiritual practice for women?

In Buddhist doctrine, there is no difference between men and women. In the vinaya as well as the bodhisattva practices, or in tantra, women can receive the highest ordination and can give the highest teachings or initiations. It is just due to social conditions that there are few women teachers. But in Tibetan history there have been many women who were very great and famous teachers. We also give the same teachings to women as to men. For example, I greatly admire my own sister. We received the same training and teachings, and we did the same retreats. Today, she is also giving the same teachings. I told her she should give more, as many people are happy to see women teachers.

If one considers everyday experience like a dream or illusion, how does one avoid nihilism?

Nihilism as I understand it just means absence, the complete opposite extreme from existence. But what we try to achieve is a realization of ultimate reality, which is above and away from all extremes, such as existing and nonexisting. To do this, first we need to establish all outer appearance as mental objects. Then we should regard all mental phenomena as a magical show. In this way, step by step, we go through the mind training.

Would you please bless us with the transmission of the essence of the Sakya lineage?

I think the best blessing is to bestow the teachings themselves, which I have just done. I have explained how to start from the basic ground, then proceed through the path up to the result, in a clear outline. So right now the best thing is to meditate together for a few moments on the teachings. That is the best way to get the transmission or blessing.

I would like to conclude this teaching by wishing you all long life, good health, and especially complete success in your spiritual path. May the blessings of the Buddha, Dharma, and Saṅgha be with you now and always. Thank you.

About the Author

His Holiness the Sakya Trichen is the forty-first head of the Sakya order of Tibetan Buddhism and a member of Tibet's noble Khon family. He is also a descendant of the five great masters who founded the Sakya order in the eleventh and twelfth centuries.

Just as His Holiness the Dalai Lama is an emanation of Avalokiteshvara, the manifestation of all the Buddhas' great compassion, His Holiness the Sakya Trichen is the emanation of Manjushri, the manifestation of all the Buddhas' transcendent wisdom.

After political changes in 1959 forced many Tibetan Buddhist leaders to leave Tibet, His Holiness reestablished the headquarters of the Sakya order in northern India. Overcoming all difficulties, he reestablished monasteries, nunneries, and colleges in India and Nepal and worked to restore the original institutions in Tibet. In short, within sixty years he accomplished not only the reestablishment of hundreds of religious institutions that had been the work of many generations of previous masters, but their expansion into new lands.

In addition to reestablishment of the Sakya order's core religious institutions and teachings, His Holiness ensured the next generation of lineage holders in the person of his highly trained and realized sons, Ratna Vajra Sakya and Gyana Vajra Sakya, who serve as the forty-second and forty-third Sakya Trizins.

During the 1970s, His Holiness began to establish Sakya centers in various countries of the world, with hundreds of centers under his guidance in the Americas, Europe, and Southeast Asia. In 2000, His Holiness established Tsechen Kunchab Ling, in Walden, New York, as his monastic seat in the Americas.

His Holiness is the peerless guide and leader of hundreds of thousands of monks, nuns, and lay students in Tibet, India, Nepal, Southeast Asia, Australia, Europe, and North America. From his main seat in Rajpur, India, he travels tirelessly throughout the world to direct the work of the temples and centers, to fulfill requests for teachings, and to benefit beings.

What to Read Next from Wisdom Publications

Freeing the Heart and Mind, Part One
Introduction to the Buddhist Path
His Holiness the Sakya Trichen

Freeing the Heart and Mind, Part Two
Chogyal Phagpa on the Buddhist Path
His Holiness the Sakya Trichen

The Sakya School of Tibetan Buddhism
Dhongthog Rinpoche
Translated by Sam van Schaik

About Wisdom Publications

Wisdom Publications is the leading publisher of classic and contemporary Buddhist books and practical works on mindfulness. To learn more about us or to explore our other books, please visit our website at wisdomexperience.org or contact us at the address below.

Wisdom Publications
199 Elm Street
Somerville, MA 02144 USA

We are a 501(c)(3) organization, and donations in support of our mission are tax deductible.

Wisdom Publications is affiliated with the Foundation for the Preservation of the Mahayana Tradition (FPMT).